£1.49

# Cron

## Interviews

Written by the staff of
Croner's Employment Law
Editorial Department

*Maureen Lyacer*
*August 1992*

## CRONER PUBLICATIONS LIMITED

Croner House, 173 Kingston Road,
New Malden, Surrey KT3 3SS

Telephone 01-942 8966

# Croner's Guide to Interviews

First Edition
April 1985
Revised Reprint March 1987

© Copyright Croner Publications Ltd.
ISBN 0 900319 36 4

# Contents

# Introduction

As a manager or supervisor of staff you would probably
be amazed if you sat down and worked out the
proportion of your time spent interviewing. There is a
tendency to believe that only recruitment interviews
count but this is far from true. Every time an employee
comes to see you about a problem or grievance, every
time you have to speak to employees about their work
performance or conduct, a customer rings to complain, a
health and safety inspector calls, you are conducting an
interview. At its simplest, it can be defined as a two-way
flow of information designed to enable both interviewer
and interviewee to decide on the most effective future
course of action.

Partly because people do not think of an 'interview' in
these terms, partly because of the widespread view that
good interviewers are born not made, many managers
are given little help in carrying out interviews
effectively.

On the other side of the coin, there are those who do
not believe they need to be given training: "I've been
doing it for years – you can't teach me anything new".
However, an interview which is not properly planned, or
where the wrong questions are asked, or even where the
right questions are asked in the wrong way, can cause
endless niggling problems: disciplinary matters are rarely
resolved at the first informal stage; appraisal interviews
always turn into battles of wits; or people who seemed
to be so good at the recruitment interview turn out to
be far short of perfect when they actually start work.

Interviews are not always easy: at times they may be
extremely stressful, but if the interviewer has done the
necessary homework there is much more chance of the
interview achieving its objective. In this guide we aim to
give advice and information on preparing for,
conducting and following up the interview in order to be
as sure as possible that any decisions resulting from it
are made on the basis of the best possible information.

# Why Interview?

There are, of course, many people who do not really believe that interviews are worth having. There is one popular story about a psychologist who persuaded an organisation to take part in an experiment. In the first year they interviewed candidates for their traineeships in the normal manner; in the second year they accepted people on a first-come basis: the failure rate in the first year was **higher** than in the second. However, it is possible that such a result says more about the standard of interviewing, or the level of motivation of the trainees, than it does about the interview itself.

It is difficult to imagine a better way of exploring people's views, attitudes, interests and so forth than to have a structured, face to face discussion with them. Reports, questionnaires, letters may all have their place, but in general they can only add to the effectiveness of the interview. They cannot adequately replace it. It is only by discussing something directly with interviewees that you have any real chance of assessing the value of the information they are giving: you can follow up statements made with probing questions to try to see whether they are giving real views or are seeking to please and you can judge a lot from their 'body language' – but do beware of reading too much into that. The interview is always somewhat artificial, particularly when it is an appraisal, disciplinary or recruitment interview as the interviewee is likely to be under some stress.

# Objectives of the Interview

For an interview to be effective, you must have a very clear idea of the objectives you are aiming to achieve. This sounds too obvious to need stating, but there are many people who, faced with some sort of problem, react by calling in a subordinate or another manager for a chat. This, though, is just an interview by another name, and as such it requires forethought and planning. Why do you need a chat? What do you hope to achieve by it? Do you need to get background information first? Are you speaking to the right person? Without asking yourself such questions beforehand, your chances of resolving the problems quickly will diminish radically.

Having established your objective as precisely as possible, this should, in almost every case, be conveyed clearly to the interviewee at the outset. Without a good idea of the purpose of the discussion, there is little likelihood of their giving you all the relevant information.

It should also be noted that, if the objective has not been clarified, an interview may not even be necessary. If all you want to do is to impart information – to keep employees informed of a new product range, to issue an instruction, etc.– then no two-way flow of information is required and so the interview is unnecessary.

## Preparation

The essential preparatory step before almost any interview is to gather together all of the relevant background information and study it carefully. For instance, in the case of a grievance interview, do you know the nature of the employee's grievance? If not, and you have no legitimate way of finding out beforehand, be prepared to adjourn the meeting once the precise nature of the grievance is known so that you can obtain the necessary advice or information from other members of the company. Where you do know the grievance and, for example, it relates to a personality clash between two employees, it is essential to know what your organisation's policy is regarding transfers between departments as this may be a possible solution.

There is also a need to pay heed to the administrative and physical arrangements for an interview.

### Administrative Arrangements

The first factor to consider is the timing of the interview. The main points to take into account are:
● is the interviewee going to have to travel to the interview? If so, it should be planned for around the middle of the day;

3

- it is often helpful when carrying out disciplinary interviews to hold them towards the end of the day to avoid the problem of employees, who may be angry and upset, disrupting work in their department when they return at the end of the meeting;

- try not to hold too many interviews in one day. There is often a desire to hold all interviews in the shortest possible time, but to interview six or more people in one day is so tiring that it is difficult to do justice to those interviewees you see at the end of the day or to remember clearly those you interviewed first thing in the morning; and

- most importantly, how urgent is the interview? Always try to get the balance right. There is often a desire to put off a difficult interview for too long, thus increasing the difficulty in most cases, or to rush in to tackle a problem without giving it due thought.

Decide who will need to participate in the interview. If there are several interested parties, consider whether their presence is likely to inhibit or intimidate the interviewee. If so, can the interviews be staged to overcome this problem? Make sure that the interviewee knows when and where the interview is to take place, its likely duration and the identity of the interviewers.

In the case of people coming from outside the company, ensure that they are given adequate directions to the premises and brief your receptionist or gatekeeper on who to expect, when and where to direct them. Then, whether the interviewees are from inside or outside the company, make sure that you are ready for them and they are not left to kick their heels for what may seem to them like hours on end.

Finally, if there is to be more than one person conducting the interview, it is useful to hold a briefing meeting to discuss strategy: particular points to be covered, who is to ask which questions, in what order and who will take any necessary notes. Also ensure that interviewers sit fairly close together, so that the interviewee is not made to behave like a spectator at Wimbledon!

## Physical Arrangements

The last point to be made regarding preparation
concerns the physical setting: a quiet room must be
available where the interview can be carried on without
interruptions. The layout of the room should be
determined by the formality of the interview. If it is to
be conducted in a relaxed, informal manner, it is better
to get away from the desk. Set chairs around a coffee
table for example, if one is available. However, whether
or not you conduct the interview from behind a desk, it
is important to make sure that all chairs are of the same
height and that there is space for the interviewee to put
any papers he might need, his coffee cup, ashtray, etc.
Incidentally, it is a good idea to spell out the ground
rules on smoking right at the start, either by offering a
cigarette or by explaining that your office is a 'no-
smoking zone' and asking them not to smoke during the
interview.

# Interview Styles

There is no one 'right' way to conduct an interview, as
so much depends on your own personality and
management style. The main point is to establish
rapport with interviewees in order to draw them out
then steer the conversation into the right channel.
Essentially, interview styles can be broken down into
five approaches.

**Tell me all about it:** the aim of this type of strategy is
to put the interviewee completely at ease – this is a
normal, everyday situation, rather than a formal and
possibly threatening experience. The interviewer is
friendly, open and genuinely interested in the
interviewee.

**Joint problem solving:** a strategy that can be of
particular use in disciplinary or grievance interviews, this
involves discussing the situation and getting the
employee's commitment to working towards a solution
which he/she has arrived at with the interviewer.

**Tell and sell:** this strategy involves the interviewer
'selling' the interviewee his own solution, through

persuasion. While it can be used to effect in some interviews it may be disastrous if used, for instance, in a selection interview, where the applicant is persuaded that he can do a particular job on the basis of a brief conversation.

**Tell and listen:** a half-way house between the preceding two strategies, this involves providing the interviewee with the relevant information, listening to his views, then guiding him towards an appropriate position.

**Stress:** this strategy is the opposite of the 'tell me all about it' approach. It requires the interviewer to challenge the employee's views, ridicule his beliefs and belittle his assumptions. While it has been argued that it is a useful way of judging people's assertiveness and/or tolerance, it can create havoc with industrial relations if used in grievance, disciplinary or appraisal interviews, and stands little chance of being effective in such cases.

The approach to be followed will depend on the type of interview being carried out and, as mentioned above, on the interviewer's personality. However, when circumstances warrant it, even the most autocratic managers should be able to train themselves to use the joint problem solving strategy. Equally important, never try to use a new interview technique unless you are sure you can handle it. This is particularly important with stress interviews which, if not undertaken by professionals, can result in valued employees walking out, or even in strikes.

## Questioning and Listening

Since the main purpose of the interview is to elicit information from the interviewee, it follows that the questions asked are of critical importance. With most interviews it will be possible to draw up a checklist of points that must be explored. This is extremely useful since it does help you to keep control of the interview. If the interviewee goes off at a tangent you will be able to bring him back to the matter in hand more easily and if each item is checked off you can be sure that, when the interview is over, you will not suddenly remember an important point that was overlooked. However, the checklist should serve only as a guide to matters you need to check out – there may well be other matters raised by the interviewee which do need to be aired. The key is to assess whether they are genuine issues or just unnecessary diversions.

Before even beginning to question you will need to set the tone of the interview. Let interviewees know how formal it is; give the necessary information to them to enable them to answer your questions sensibly and, where possible, make them feel at ease by commenting on the weather, their journey, etc.

In actually asking the questions, the following points should be borne in mind:

● always ask the questions in a logical sequence – for instance working through a matter chronologically;

● avoid multiple questions, for example: "What are your qualifications for this job? How long have you been doing it and what do you enjoy most about it?" Such a question may well confuse interviewees and, where qualifications are important, will offer unqualified people a chance of ducking the central issue by launching into a tale about their long experience, enthusiasm, etc;

● ask open questions, not ones that require an answer of "yes" or "no". For instance: "What do you enjoy most about your current job?" instead of: "Do you enjoy your job?";

● give interviewees time to think about their answers. Never think that you must rush in with a supplementary question just because there is a pause in the conversation;

● probe answers to important questions, to check their accuracy and to obtain important details;

● summarise the course of the interview regularly to ensure that agreement has been achieved on all important issues.

Finally, make sure that you listen carefully to interviewees' replies.

asy to assume that everyone with reasonable
h.. ng can listen effectively but, sadly, this is far from
true. One of the main problems is lack of concentration
on what the interviewee is saying and there are a variety
of reasons for this:

- thinking of what your next question is to be while the
  interviewee is speaking;
- allowing your own prejudices to lead you to draw
  faulty inferences from answers, or jumping to
  unjustified conclusions;
- conducting too many interviews in one day, or
  interviewing when your mind is preoccupied by other
  concerns, so that you are unable to concentrate fully;
  and
- jumping to conclusions, and so putting words into
  interviewees' mouths, rather than allowing them to
  develop their answer fully.

Going back to an earlier section of this chapter, good
preparation beforehand will help to overcome many of
these problems and practice will improve your listening
skills even if it does not lead to total perfection!

An important aspect of good listening is to make
interviewees feel that what they have to say is
important, that you are interested in what their views
are. Again, preparation will help: you will have
prepared the right environment, will have ensured there
will be no interruptions and will have allowed sufficient
time so that interviewees do not feel they are taking up
your valuable time unnecessarily.

## Evaluating the Interview

So, having asked the right questions and listened
carefully to the answers, you then have to evaluate the
information you have obtained. It is always better not to
rely on your memory: there is nothing wrong with
making brief notes during the interview. Indeed, many
interviewees will positively welcome your noting down
important points as it means that you have appreciated
their significance.

As soon as possible after the interview, you should amplify your notes, analyse their significance – bearing in mind your own views and prejudices – and then consider the outcome of the interview compared with your original objectives. You will then be in a position to follow up with appropriate action, depending on the type of interview.

## The Legal Aspects

Lastly, before turning to the dos and don'ts of specific interviews, it is worth looking at the legal aspects of interviews. The main areas here are sex and race discrimination. Asking questions of a woman such as: "Do you think men would resent having to work for a woman?" or "Don't you think this is really a man's job?" may well lead her to believe that you are discriminating against her on the grounds of her sex and could result in a tribunal claim being made against you and/or your company.

This point will be dealt with more fully in succeeding chapters, but the ground rules for avoiding discriminatory questions are quite simple: ask only for information which is necessary to enable you to meet the objectives of the interview, and ask only questions to which you can expect a reasonable and honest reply. For instance, it is absurd (as well as potentially discriminatory) to ask a young woman who is applying for a job, promotion, training course, etc. whether or not she intends to have a baby in the near future. If that is her intention, she is unlikely to prejudice her chances by saying so and, in any event, it is unlikely that a woman with such imminent plans would be applying for the job or the promotion!

Incidentally, throughout this book and for the sake of simplicity, the word 'he' is used instead of the more clumsy 's/he'.

Finally, all interviewers should be aware of the basic elements of contract law, since this can have important implications; it is all too easy to end a selection, grievance or counselling interview by making an offer of employment or an offer to vary the terms of contract of an existing employee. You should be aware that, in general terms, once such an offer is made and accepted, it is binding on the company. Going back to the employee the next day to say "Sorry, I've discovered that I cannot let you have that pay increase in return for your offer to work in unpleasant surroundings" will cut very little ice. The employee could make a claim for damages in respect of breach of contract to the County Court.

Another aspect of contract law to bear in mind is the Misrepresentation Act 1967, which provides that if someone enters into a contract after its terms have been misrepresented to him – and suffers damage as a result – he can claim damages in the County Court or High Court.

# Selection Interviews

Although the interview is used for a number of purposes in the employment field, the selection or job interview is, for many people, the one with which they are most familiar. Virtually everyone has been on the receiving end of one at some time or other, and few people would expect to be offered employment without having been interviewed first. This is not to say that such a practice does not occur, but certainly for most employers the idea of choosing a new member of staff without any form of interview whatsoever borders on the unthinkable. In this respect, the interview has become the most common and accepted method of selecting people for work.

So what exactly is a selection interview and what is its purpose? Basically it is an exchange of information between the candidate and the employer. It can range from a simple conversation about rates of pay, work experience, etc. to a highly structured discussion of the candidate's background and motivation, along with a more detailed analysis of the terms of employment. The former approach would normally occur where the employer is recruiting unskilled or semi-skilled labour; the latter where the vacant position is of a more senior nature.

The purpose of the selection interview from the employer's viewpoint is to investigate the background history of job applicants in order to try and predict whether they will be able to do the job to the required standard. In other words, it is first and foremost a means of gathering information on which to base a decision. However, the job interview also provides a means of enabling candidates to see whether or not the job is right for them – a factor which becomes increasingly important as one moves up the scale of seniority. On a mutual basis, the interview is also an important stage in the formation of a contract of employment. It acts as the forum where many of the terms of the contract are discussed and agreed between the employer and the prospective employee. Therefore, the job interview acts as a means of selection from both the employer's viewpoint and that of the candidate to enable both parties to undertake a matching process – to see whether or not they suit each other.

## The Preliminaries

Obviously, before any interviews can be held it is necessary to have undertaken a recruitment exercise to provide a shortlist of candidates for selection. It is not within the scope of this book to carry out a comprehensive examination of techniques of recruitment; this chapter is only concerned with the role of the interview as a part of the selection process. Suffice it to say, even in the case of the most mundane and unskilled job, you should attempt to identify the requirements of the job and develop some idea of the type of person to best fit those requirements. This will help to establish which candidates you wish to interview.

To do this, a systematic approach should be adopted. Ideally a job description, accurately reflecting the purpose, duties and responsibilities of the work and the working conditions, should be compiled. Secondly, a specification of the ideal type of person who would be able to do the job to the right standard should be drawn up. This should specify the knowledge or skills required, education, training, qualifications, experience, etc. and any other specific requirements such as age, location and physical characteristics. Once compiled, this can be used as the standard against which candidates are compared.

Although the personnel specification is probably the most important aid to successful selection, there are still some managers who undertake selection interviewing with nothing more than a vague idea of the type of person they are looking for. This inevitably results in a decision being taken to offer the 'wrong' person the job. The manager who makes no attempt to identify his needs in this way before undertaking the interviewing process is usually the first to complain that the appointed candidate "can't do the job" or "doesn't measure up". So, the message is clear: even for the simplest of jobs it is a worthwhile exercise to use the tasks involved to establish a 'blueprint' of the ideal job-holder.

In addition, before conducting a job interview a certain amount of information will need to be available to the interviewer so that a preliminary matching process can be undertaken. In most cases the candidate's letter of application, completed application form, or curriculum vitae will provide the basis for this process. Even in cases where a candidate has applied by telephone, any notes taken at the time, recording brief details of the candidate's background, can be put to good use. Obviously, where applicants have been instructed to apply in person and no written form of application is used, the interview will have to commence without prior consideration of the candidate's background. However, such instances will normally be confined to short-term unskilled appointments where the need for prior information is more limited.

From the information available in advance, no-hopers can be weeded out and a shortlist of candidates compiled by considering individual applications in conjunction with the personnel specification. It is, of course, very unlikely that you will ever recruit the 'ideal' candidate but the requirements of the personnel specification should be matched as closely as possible.

## Preparing to Interview

It is important that thorough preparation for the interview is undertaken by the employer to enable the process to be effective and to run without hitches.

**Notifying candidates:** first of all, it will be necessary to establish when and where the interview will be conducted and to invite the candidates in good time so that other arrangements can be made if, for any reason, a particular applicant cannot attend at the time specified. Give the candidate some idea as to how long the interview will last, the name of a person to report to on arrival, whether the company will reimburse travelling expenses, etc.

**Timetable:** the appointments' schedule should allow enough time to be thorough and to cover the ground systematically. Even where the need to fill vacancies is particularly pressing, it is better to leave too much time between appointments rather than too little. A discussion which has reached a critical stage, but is then ended abruptly due to time restrictions, will not give you much scope to select objectively and will leave the candidate feeling let down. Similarly, keeping people waiting for long periods while an interview is painstakingly drawn out to time will not create a good impression. It is important to remember that it is the candidates' time as well as your own and they may have just as many demands on it as you do.

**Interviewers:** depending on the nature of the job, you may wish to involve more than one person in the interviewing process – typically where the job holder will be required to report to more than one boss, or you feel that obtaining more than one opinion on the suitability of the applicant will reduce the likelihood of bias. This can be achieved either by having a series of separate interviews with different individuals, for example where the personnel department holds a screening interview which is followed by a more job-related discussion with a departmental head, or by using a panel of managers to conduct a joint interview. The latter has the advantage of saving time and gives everyone the opportunity of seeing the candidate in the same situation. However this degree of formality is not conducive to conversation and the success of such interviews depends largely on the ability of the panel to act as a unit. Where more than one interviewer is being used, make sure those involved are notified of the date, time, venue, etc. in good time.

**Surroundings:** attention should be paid to the physical setting of the interview. If a candidate can feel completely at ease in the environment, conversation will flow more easily: the purpose, remember, is to encourage a full exchange of information. First of all, somewhere quiet will be needed where you will not be disturbed. Make arrangements not to be interrupted. Phone calls and people descending on the interview will not impress the candidate and will inhibit the flow. Pay attention to the seating arrangements. Do not use chairs which are so restrictive that candidates cannot move once they sit down, or which are likely to collapse under somebody of above average weight. It is generally best to avoid using a desk to separate the interviewer from the applicant as this creates a more formal atmosphere with the desk acting as a barrier to relaxed conversation. However, if one is used make sure it is uncluttered and arrange the seating so that candidates are not placed directly opposite the interviewer as though they are about to begin a game of chess. Perhaps the best solution is to arrange chairs around a coffee table.

Finally, ensure that the usual social courtesies are observed. See that space is available where the candidate's coat, briefcase, etc. can be placed and, if you are happy to let candidates smoke, provide them with an ashtray.

**Planning interview strategy:** before the interview begins it is important that you familiarise yourself with all the documents which will have a bearing on the selection process. A thorough read through the job description and personnel specification will refresh the memory, and a detailed study of the individual's application will enable interview strategy to be planned. Areas about which you specifically wish to question the candidate should be identified: gaps in employment history, reasons for leaving particular jobs, health, etc. Look for clues: a long gap between two periods of stable employment might indicate a bona fide period of unemployment or study leave, or it might indicate a period of detention at Her Majesty's pleasure. Look out for vague, general statements: "reponsible for main accounts work conducted in the office" could reasonably imply control of all the company's financial dealings, or, if the office referred to means the person's own department, it may mean that the individual's sole function is to pay out expenses from the petty cash box.

Highlighting specific points on which you wish to question the candidate will enable you to determine the line of questioning which you intend to adopt. Where a panel or separate interviews are being used it is useful to have a meeting of interviewers beforehand to go through the documents together and decide the sequence of questions and topics to be covered to avoid repetition of the same material.

## Candidate Reception

It is not unreasonable for candidates arriving for interview to expect that people will know when and why they are coming. Surprisingly, many employers omit to tell those with whom they will first come into contact that interviews have been arranged and certain people will be arriving at certain times. You should always make sure that receptionists or gatekeepers are made aware of appointments and ensure that they are informed where to direct the arriving applicants. There is nothing worse than turning up for interview and being treated with anything from mild surprise to an expression which implies that you are trespassing on the premises.

The timetabling of interview schedules will normally mean that, for the candidate, some period of waiting is inevitable before the interview commences. This should be kept to the absolute minimum and waiting areas should be made as congenial as possible, preferably with comfortable seating and an adequate supply of reading matter. Perching somebody on the edge of a workbench for half an hour while the foreman sees to a minor problem does not inspire confidence or do much for the company's image. It is often a good idea to deal with any remaining administrative arrangements at this stage, e.g. travelling expenses can be seen to, additional material such as examination certificates and references can be collected from the candidate and checked over.

It is not usually a good idea to instruct all candidates to arrive for interview at the same time and then keep them waiting as each is seen in turn. The justification for this normally boils down to bureaucratic procedure as much as anything else, and there are distinct disadvantages in this approach. Firstly, distractions as important as 'the opposition' do nothing to help individual candidates to compose themselves and relax, thus restricting the chances of uninhibited discussion during the interview. Secondly, people are kept waiting for unnecessarily long periods and, finally, such a procedure can, in cases where applicants return to the waiting area after interview, result in their comparing notes about the interviewer's technique and the types of question asked. This gives subsequent interviews a rather artificial taint.

## Opening the Interview

Right from the point where you first meet candidates you should be trying to establish rapport with them in order to help them relax and to get them to talk. The emphasis is on putting each candidate at ease, by using a polite, friendly manner; perform the necessary introductions, shake hands with the candidate and guide him to his seat. Confine your opening remarks to easy, non-controversial topics: "Did you have any difficulty finding our offices?" "How did you travel here today?" If all else fails, fall back on the traditional opener to any conversation between people who have not met before: "Isn't the weather dreadful at the moment!"

Though somewhat contrived, such initial contact is comforting to the candidate and breaks the ice. A curt "You're here about the job, are you?" apart from stating the obvious does not help anyone to relax. If, while speaking, you maintain eye contact, candidates will inevitably respond – if only because they are relieved that the interview has commenced and the period of waiting in anticipation is over.

Follow up the candidate's replies and show interest in them. The interviewer who asks for an opinion on the weather and then proceeds to look away and shuffle papers while the reply is given will not establish rapport in any sense. Having 'tested the water' it is useful then to outline briefly the purpose of the meeting and the particular sequence it will take. If, for example, you prefer to leave candidates' questions until the end, tell them that this is what you propose to do, otherwise you risk their leaping in with questions at various points in the discussion which upsets the flow. Even where the interview is relatively unstructured it helps everyone to know at which point the provision of information will change emphasis.

## Questioning Techniques

Perhaps the most overlooked point in adopting a particular line of questioning is not 'what to ask' but 'where to begin' in relation to the candidate's background. The simplest approach is to adopt a chronological sequence of questions using a particular starting point in relation to the candidate's written application to keep the interview orderly. For example, where older candidates are being interviewed, do not waste too much time on an analysis of their school record or their very first job unless this is obviously relevant. Similarly, when interviewing school leavers, educational achievements will be important matters on which to concentrate. So, set the point from which questions will commence and work through systematically. Discussion can then focus on the key issues which you wish to investigate in more depth.

### Use of Questions

When conducting the interview itself it is always preferable to use 'open' questions – those which begin with what, where, why, when and how – and invite a full answer:

● "What were your responsibilities in that particular job?"
● "Why do you think that particular course was useful to you?"
● "How did that affect your prospects of promotion?"

Such questions will enable the interviewer to elicit revealing answers as they will encourage applicants to speak more freely about their background. Replies to particular questions can then be followed up through supplementary questioning. Where the response is sketchy you should probe for further information by asking direct questions which pin the candidate down to the point. For example: "You say that you left XYZ Ltd because of redundancy, but why exactly were you selected to go?"

If the candidate is trying to conceal that his previous misconduct or poor job performance were criteria for redundancy selection, this will mean that the interviewee is put on the spot: either he explains truthfully or he lies! He no longer has the option of a general statement to account for the termination of his previous employment.

In addition to using open questions, you will inevitably, at some stage, have to ask some closed questions. These are those which demand a terse "yes" or "no" answer: "Did you supervise staff in your last job?" "Presumably, you play golf regularly?" Though it is almost impossible to avoid asking any closed questions at all, they should be kept to a minimum. A long series of them will not be conducive to conversation and will not elicit a great deal of information.

In adopting particular questioning techniques it is important to remember that the interview is essentially a controlled conversation to enable an exchange of information to take place. It is not, and should not be used as, an interrogation session. By all means question the candidate thoroughly but do not turn the entire exercise into an inquisition.

Introducing an element of stress into the proceedings is usually unnecessary unless it is important to assess the way in which people react under pressure. For example, in certain jobs the ability to remain calm and resist argument is an essential requirement, e.g. airline pilots or sales representatives operating in a highly competitive environment. Even in such cases, stress tactics such as aggressive questioning or the use of disparaging reports should be employed with caution. Most managers and supervisors are not trained psychologists and are in no real position to evaluate behaviour objectively when stress is applied deliberately. The use of stress to 'see what he's made of' is therefore something to be discouraged unless the situation warrants it.

Leading questions or those which tend to reveal which answer the interviewer expects should also be avoided. "Would you agree with me that timekeeping is essential

in a job like this?" "You do accept that, don't you?"
There really is only one answer for the candidate to give
to this type of question and they invariably achieve
little. Even if the candidate does agree that timekeeping
is important, does this mean that he is any more likely
to be punctual and reliable?

Multiple questions are also not to be encouraged as
they tend to confuse the candidate who will not know
which to answer first. For example: "Were you
responsible for many staff and how did you get on with
your boss?" This, at best, will result in the interviewee
asking you which he should begin with; at worst it will
provoke a garbled answer based on a mixture of the
two.

## Legal Provisions

Under the Sex Discrimination and Race Relations Acts
it is unlawful to discriminate against job applicants on
grounds of sex, marital status or racial origin, etc.
Questions asked during interviews may show an
intention to discriminate if they reflect assumptions about
one particular group, or if they are only asked of
women or of men or of certain racial groups. For
example, to ask women whether they intend to get
married or to start a family might not be discriminatory
in itself if it is a genuine requirement of the job that
employees are single and remain childless, and if the
same question is asked of men; for example where it is
necessary for the job-holder to live on the premises and
it is not possible to provide accommodation other than
for a single person. However, even where both men and
women are asked this question it may still be
discriminatory if the reason for requesting the
information is based on the assumption that, once
married and/or having had children, the woman will
leave because her husband will automatically become
the breadwinner.

In essence, then, it is important that there is a good
reason for asking the question in the first place. Where
employers are concerned that a potential employee
should be able to meet the requirements of the job, e.g.

travelling or staying away from home overnight, they can and should check the candidate's domestic commitments. However, they must ensure that no discriminatory assumptions are made.

The Rehabilitation of Offenders Act also prohibits employers from asking ex-offenders, whose convictions are spent (i.e. when a specified period has elapsed since the date of the conviction), whether they have had a spent conviction (except in certain exempted professions). Also, if an employer asks a rehabilitated offender if he has a criminal record, the candidate is entitled to deny this if it has become spent in accordance with the Act.

**Encouraging Response and Listening**

Interviewers must not, of course, confine their attention purely to asking questions. Encouraging the candidate to respond to them and to expand on what initially may be short, nervous answers is an essential element of successful interviewing. The use of silence to give interviewees time to think and to encourage them to expand on their initial response to a particular question is a simple technique which can be used effectively. Similarly, maintaining eye contact, nodding, and looking interested in the content of the candidates' replies will keep them talking. The use of encouraging noises – "uh-huh!" etc. – will also assist the process.

You must make sure that you listen to the replies given to you. Sadly, many interviewers see their role purely in terms of asking questions and fail to do the one thing which is crucial – listen to the answers! Listening is not the same as hearing. It involves a more conscious assimilation of information and requires attentiveness on the part of the interviewer. Failure to listen properly to what the candidate is saying will mean that probing questions cannot be put to effective use and the interview may become a worthless exercise.

In listening to replies, you must also assess and evaluate them so that follow up questions can be asked and further information gained. A certain amount of evaluation should take place after the interview so it is a good idea to take **brief** notes while the candidate is talking. A balance should be struck between illegible jottings which mean absolutely nothing to the interviewer after the candidate has departed, and a transcript of everything that has been said which will not only slow the interview down but will also flummox most candidates!

Notes can be taken either on the application form itself adjoining information already provided by the applicant or through the use of an interview assessment form whereby the personnel specification can be used as a guide against which specific information can be noted down.

## Retaining Control

As an interviewer you should not allow the interview to run out of control. A candidate who has become sufficiently relaxed to talk at length on every question which is asked must be carefully and consciously steered back to the point if too many irrelevancies creep into the conversation. Similarly, a candidate who tries to take over and dominate the proceedings must be checked. It may be necessary to employ specific tactics to bring the conversation back to the point.

One method of doing this is to ask a series of closed questions. This stems the tide to quite a degree as it forces the candidate to reply briefly. Breaking eye contact to look at the application form can sometimes help. If all else fails, it may be necessary to interrupt the candidate if he is particularly voluble; ask him to answer briefly, or even tell him that his point is not relevant. Candidates who do not respond to the earlier signals are few, but it is sometimes necessary to adopt extreme tactics to steer the discussion back on course.

## Closing the Interview

In cases where the interview has gone according to plan, the interviewer should now be in receipt of sufficient information about the candidate on which to base his decision. However, it must be remembered that the interview is a two-way process and provision of information from the interviewer to the interviewee is of vital importance. Particular points about the job itself will inevitably have been discussed through the questioning process but it is very important that the interviewee is given the opportunity to ask questions of the interviewer. This is where familiarity with the job description and terms of employment becomes essential: the manager who cannot remember particular aspects of the work or the rates of pay and benefits provided will quickly sink in the candidate's estimation. Remember, the interview is as much a device to enable the candidate to see if he wants the job and to discuss the terms of employment, as it is a selection device for the employer.

Another point to note is that it is important that the job is represented accurately to the candidate. Dressing up a mundane job to sound stimulating and challenging is a waste of everybody's time: the candidate who accepts it on this basis will probably leave very quickly due to boredom with the job. Similarly, jobs which demand a great deal from the employee should be treated in the same way. Terms of employment must also be represented accurately. A failure to be precise can result in a candidate accepting a job offer on misrepresented terms. If this occurs the employee will be quite entitled to enforce the terms if the employer subsequently wishes to change them unilaterally.

When discussions have been completed it is up to the interviewer to terminate the process smoothly – the candidate will rarely leave until he is invited to. Gather your papers together, round off the discussion by checking to see whether the candidate has anything further to ask and, assuming there are no further points, close the interview by thanking the candidate for his time and explaining to him the next step in the procedure, i.e. whether there will be a second interview, when he will be notified, etc. Finally, stand up, invite the candidate to collect his belongings and show him out.

## Evaluation

Whilst a great deal of the evaluation of information

obtained during the interview will be carried out at the point when it is received, it is necessary to consider the information fully after the candidate has left. Make use of the personnel specification and any notes taken during the course of the discussion to assess the candidate's suitability. These notes will also be useful if a claim of sex or race discrimination is made by an unsuccessful candidate.

Remember, the personnel specification provides the guideline against which the information should be assessed. It is not appropriate to view selection interviewing as a means of selecting the 'best of the bunch'. Whilst comparisons between candidates will inevitably be made, do not lose sight of the fact that the standard is the 'ideal' contained in the personnel specification. If the whole bunch are not up to this standard, picking the best one will not result in successful selection. Hopefully, this situation will arise only rarely. If it does, though, you really must start all over again.

# Appraisal Interviews

Appraisal, for some people, is a dirty word. For the employee, it might mean that dreaded time every year when the manager makes the most of his chance to 'have a go' at him. Or, at the other extreme, it may just have become a meaningless annual ritual which never seems to lead to anything in the way of change or improvement – it is probably never even referred to again. It can be disliked equally by the manager, who hates the idea of having to confront his subordinates with their failings, or who resents having to carry out an exercise which he considers to be a total waste of his valuable time.

Needless to say, this sort of approach to the appraisal interview can only have pretty disastrous results. Yet still the appraisals are carried out, year in and year out, because somebody in the organisation believes they are 'a good thing' – and so they can be, providing they are carried out effectively. Benefits can be reaped by the appraised, the appraiser and the organisation in terms of increased commitment from the employee, the highlighting of areas of confusion or ambiguity, the identification of people with potential and the establishment of training needs.

## Purpose of Appraisal

Some of the problems with appraisal arise simply because those involved see its purpose only in terms of determining how much the salary increase will be, filling in the form or telling employees where they went wrong. Certainly, these may all play a part in appraisal but there is always the danger of 'just going through the motions' when it is seen in that light. To be effective it needs to encompass much more. Insofar as the link with pay is concerned, it makes more sense to separate the two issues, especially as this allows the employee to make any necessary improvements before the pay review is carried out.

Essentially, appraisal is a means of measuring or assessing performance. To be effective it should incorporate a combination of such aims as:

- identifying the employee's strengths and weaknesses;
- highlighting problem areas or those requiring improvement;
- employee motivation;
- maintaining or improving work standards;
- recognising and encouraging good work;
- identifying training and/or development needs;
- discovering employees' ambitions;
- assessing potential for promotion or development;
- encouraging and improving communication between manager and subordinate;
- distributing rewards such as pay, status, power.

## Why Bother with an Interview?

Having got this far, one response might be: "OK, I accept that appraisal can have its uses, but why the need for a special interview?" If appraisal is going to get anywhere near meeting the aims set out above it must be based on all the relevant information available. The two main sources of such information are likely to be the employee in question and his manager, so that some means of getting the employee's information from him must be devised. It could be argued that the completion of a form or questionnaire might meet that need.

However, what makes the interview the most appropriate forum is that appraisal should be a two-way process. It is important that the employee knows what his boss thinks of his work and his prospects. If areas for improvement are to be pointed out it is only fair to tell the person concerned how to go about making the improvements. Similarly, he should have the right to protest about an assessment if he disagrees with it.

Those who argue against appraisal interviews generally fall into two groups. Firstly, there are those who acknowledge the need for this two-way communication on job performance, but deny the requirement for a formal approach via interviews. For one thing, they argue, a good supervisor or manager should be carrying out all the various strands of appraisal on a day-to-day basis, constantly communicating with his subordinates about their work. Where this is the case it makes an annual formal appraisal that much easier and more effective, but there are dangers in seeing it as an alternative to the formal interview. There may be important matters which have so far gone unsaid because the opportunity to bring them up has not arisen; the supervisor may have gained an inaccurate impression of the employee's view of his work situation; or the manager's opinion that he communicates well with his subordinates may not actually be one that is held by the employees themselves. If nothing else, the interview will provide an opportunity for both parties to review the last year or so, consolidate their impressions and views and raise any outstanding issues. For some companies it has achieved its purpose if it does nothing more than to ensure that each employee is spoken to about his work at least once a year!

Another argument against appraisal interviews put forward by this group is that, if they are to be done properly, time must be taken out from their important day-to-day work – too much time. Also, those managers who have large numbers of staff, or who are physically remote from them, may not see enough of their subordinates or know enough about their work to carry out a worthwhile appraisal interview. In the short term, and with new employees, the first of these arguments may be valid to some extent, but it is a rather short-sighted approach. Surely one of the long-term benefits of appraisal could be a smooth-running department staffed with motivated employees, making the manager's day-to-day job easier anyway. As for the second point, bearing in mind that one of the aims of appraisal is improved communication, the discipline of a formal interview may be what is needed to start closing the gap between such a manager and his subordinates.

The more common reasons for the dislike of appraisal interviews are those which are not openly voiced or readily admitted. The key factor is really a part of human nature: people do not like to judge others and criticise them face to face. It often causes embarrassment on the part of the manager and is frequently the reason for ineffective appraisal – when the appraiser 'chickens out' of telling the employee what he really needs to know. It is never pleasant or easy to discuss an employee's shortcomings with him, but providing it is done positively and constructively it is an essential part of getting the most out of the workforce – and for them to get the most out of their jobs. Similarly, if the reluctance to carry out an appraisal interview is because of some problem with the working relationship – conflict or a grudge, for instance – the sooner it is brought out into the open and discussed the sooner it can be resolved. The anticipation of such a 'show-down' often turns out to be much worse than the actual event, and the longer such problems are left to smoulder the more difficult it is likely to be to put out the fire once it is finally tackled.

Another difficulty arises in respect of people in declining industries or in 'dead-end' jobs: what is the use of appraisal in such circumstances? At the very least, the appraisal should aim to resolve work-related problems and contribute to the employee's development – even if that development may have to take place in another organisation.

## Preparing for the Interview

There can be no excuse for failing to prepare properly for an appraisal interview since, unlike grievance interviews for instance, it is initiated by management. In fact, if the advance preparation has not been done for some reason it is probably better to postpone the interview rather than go ahead with it on an ill-prepared basis.

An important part of the preliminary preparation concerns not only the manager but also the employee who is to be appraised. It is essential to inform employees in advance so that they can prepare themselves for the interview. A week to ten days' notice is probably best. They should be told the purpose of the meeting, when and where it is to be held, how long it will last, what it will cover, how it will benefit them, etc. A pre-interview briefing may help, particularly if it is an employee's first formal appraisal or if you want him to give some thought to a particular subject which he wants to discuss. He should be encouraged to think about his job performance – any problems or difficulties he is facing, what he enjoys most or least, what his aspirations or ambitions are – and be ready to discuss these matters at the meeting. Getting the employee to fill in his own appraisal form may assist this process, but it should only be needed to help him organise his own thoughts and as a basis for discussion, rather than being kept as any kind of permanent record. The employee should at least be advised to write down his thoughts, views and any points he wishes to raise, otherwise something important might be missed.

**Prior to Interview**

When it comes to each individual interview there are a number of things which the manager should prepare in advance, including:

- location: as with other types of interview, the appraisal should be held somewhere where complete privacy can be ensured, without risk of interruption;

- timing: the interview should obviously be held at a mutually convenient time, but try to avoid a period when there is some sort of crisis affecting the employee's work – this could easily overshadow everything else;

- purpose and scope: if a time limit is to be set on the interview, say an hour, some advance thought must be given to the purpose of the meeting, particularly if special emphasis is to be put on one of the aims outlined earlier in this chapter. Similarly, it can be a mistake to try to cram everything into a one-hour session if it would be more appropriate to discuss salary or promotion at a second, follow-up interview;

- structure: tied to considerations of scope are those of what sequence the discussion will follow, especially if there is a particularly difficult issue to be covered –

timing its introduction into the session could make all the difference. A detailed structure is not necessary, just a few notes as to the order in which different areas are to be tackled. Neither should it be absolutely rigid; it is just there as a guideline which can be deviated from if need be once the interview is under way. Some sort of agenda may also be useful, particularly if the employee is asked whether he wants anything to go on it – a specific issue he wants to discuss, for instance.

**Documentation**

All the above will be a waste of time if, by the time the interview comes around, the manager does not have all the information he needs at his fingertips. Relevant documentation could include:

- job description;
- rating scales;
- performance standards;
- employee records;
- reports from colleagues, customers and others who have contact with the employee;
- any documentation necessary to support criticism;
- copies of previous appraisal forms;
- a report form, and
- (possibly) a self-assessment form from the employee.

Of course, it is not enough just to assemble these documents and give them a cursory glance immediately before the interview. They should be read carefully, the performance standards considered and notes made as to how the employee appears to be shaping up to them. The manager can use the report form as a 'trial run' to clarify his thoughts. It might be seen as his report on the employee, but he must be wary of going into the interview with a closed mind as a result of completing it: it is better for the final report form to be drawn up as a consolidation of the manager's views, the employee's views and the discussions that take place at the interview.

With all this information on both the job and the

employee now to hand, and having given the whole matter considerable thought, the manager should now be ready to conduct the interview.

## The Interview

An appraisal interview can be approached in a wide variety of ways, depending on its purpose, the work situation and the personalities of the manager and employee involved.

Generally speaking, though, an overall joint problem-solving approach is the most constructive and effective for appraisal interviews. What the manager will probably find is that during the interview his role will switch from time to time, taking in a combination of some or all of the following: adviser/analyst/assessor/ counsellor/diplomat/mentor/persuader/sympathetic listener.

The mix will be different from one appraisal to another, but the ground rules for the interview are basically the same.

### The Preliminaries

To make the most of an appraisal interview it is important to get off on the right foot. The interviewer's first objective should be to put the employee at ease and establish some sort of rapport with him, otherwise the whole exercise is likely to be a waste of time. Simple things like the seating arrangements can make a lot of difference here. For instance, with the joint problem-solving approach, an 'across-the-table' interview is likely to be less effective than less formal 'side-by-side' seating. Also, if the supervisor and employee see each other socially or have any other connection or relationship outside work, the supervisor should make it clear which 'hat' he is wearing at the interview. This will be necessary if the social relationship is not to be damaged as a result of what is said during the appraisal, particularly if some straight talking is required.

It is only natural for someone to be apprehensive about a meeting with his boss when he knows his job performance is going to be discussed and that he will hear what his boss thinks of him. If day-to-day communication between the manager and his subordinate is good, the interview is more likely to take the form of a review of past discussions, and the employee will probably have a pretty good idea what his boss thinks of his work anyway. Nevertheless, he is still likely to be nervous, bearing in mind that this formal appraisal will be 'on the record'.

You should, therefore, set the general tone of the interview at an early stage, and it should be seen as constructive by both of you, regardless of the fact that the employee's weaknesses will also be covered. The purpose of appraisal, and of that particular interview, should be explained, along with the benefits which can be reaped from it by all concerned. The organisation's own system should be described, especially if the whole process ties in with rating or pay scales. Such explanations and descriptions are all the more important where the employee is being appraised for the first time, either in the company as a whole or by you as his manager.

If the interview is to follow an established sequence or be structured in any particular way, e.g. if the employee's weaknesses are to be discussed first, and then his strengths, this should be pointed out to him in advance. (For the pros and cons of a structured approach see below.)

Some interviewers also like, at this stage, to give the employee an indication of the overall impression they have gained of his work, i.e. favourable or unfavourable, so setting the scene for what is to come. Take care though, if the general assessment is unfavourable, not to put the employee so much on the defensive that nothing constructive can be done to put matters right. At the end of this preliminary stage, the interviewer should at least have some idea of what sort of reaction he is likely to get from the employee during the rest of the interview.

## Getting down to the Nitty Gritty

One cardinal sin of which some appraisers, particularly

the reluctant ones, are guilty, is to allow the preliminaries to go on and on to the extent that they take up most of the interview. Usually this is because they want to put off until as late as possible that dreaded moment when they must tell the employee where he is going wrong. At some point in the effective appraisal interview, though, you must get down to the nitty gritty of discussing what the employee is doing well or not so well and – as long as all the **necessary** preliminaries have been dealt with – the sooner the better.

What puts many appraisers off at this point is not knowing how to deal with this part of the interview. Which should you cover first, the good points or the bad points? Any opportunity to put off having to do the unpleasant part will probably be jumped at, and so it is a fairly natural inclination for the interviewer to start off by dealing with the employee's strong points. This has the advantage of helping put the employee at ease and getting the interview well under way. The drawbacks can include a tendency for the employee to be too busy anticipating the criticisms to pay attention to the first part, and there is also the danger that the session will end on a bad note, possibly distorting the employee's overall impression of the interview.

The reverse process of weaknesses followed by strengths can also cause problems, particularly if the manager overcompensates with the praise to try and sugar the pill of criticisms he has just given. The employee can easily leave the interview having almost forgotten his deficiencies, or at least feeling that they are so outweighed by his strengths that they are not worth worrying about.

Some interviewers attempt to solve these problems by using what is commonly known as 'the sandwich method', i.e. each criticism is followed by praise. The effect on the employee, though, can be pretty damaging. He will start to hear every piece of praise in terms of "You do an excellent job in this respect, but . . .". The overall impact is for the good points to be constantly overshadowed by the bad, making a constructive joint approach to problems difficult to achieve.

Of course, most of the drawbacks described can be countered effectively by a comprehensive summing up session at the end of the interview (see below), but there are a couple of other alternatives available. One involves using the structure of the job or work pattern as a guide. Providing the job description is accurate and up-to-date, each task and aspect of the job can be discussed in the order listed, regardless of the employee's performance in respect of it. Alternatively, the various parts of the job may be dealt with in order of importance, again regardless of how well they are performed.

The other option is to get the employee to start talking about the job and encourage him to identify his strengths and weaknesses. They can then be cross-checked against the interviewer's own pre-prepared list of what he would like to see the discussion cover or bring out.

Whichever approach is adopted, the aim at this stage of the interview is to promote a discussion about all parts of the job. A two-way flow of information is essential and you should constantly be checking that the information you have does comprise a full account of the employee's work and performance and comparing his observations and opinions with your own.

The employee should be encouraged to express his views and question your assessment where he considers it unjust. Finding out how he feels about the job – which bits he likes best, which bits are boring, what he thinks of his pay and other rewards, and what his hopes are for the future in terms of work – can provide a very useful insight into some of his problems and how to solve them. More pay is seldom the whole answer!

If the employee can be encouraged to identify his own strengths and weaknesses, and they more or less match your view of his work, all well and good. The next task is to agree the problem areas with him and to get him thinking positively about solving them. If he has recognised the problems for himself this whole process will be a lot easier. Unfortunately, appraisal is not always that straightforward and you may need to play a much more active role at this stage. It may be up to you to point out the employee's strengths and weaknesses as you see them, either because he is not prepared to acknowledge them readily or really does not see them in the same light.

Do not forget that appraisal is a two-way process: just as you can gain useful information from the employee, so can it work the other way. All too often employees are left unaware of the importance in their manager's eyes of some aspect of the job, do not give it much attention, and so a problem develops between them and their manager. Appraisal interviews can clear up such problems and, after all, one of the aims of appraisal is to let the employee know where he stands in terms of his performance.

If the ball is placed in your court in this way, you should try to concentrate on facts rather than personality, be objective rather than judgmental. Your job is to get the employee to agree the problem areas with you, and one of the best ways of doing that is to give specific instances rather than making general statements. For example, with a supervisor who is having problems managing his subordinates effectively because he has only recently been promoted from among their ranks and feels the need to be liked, be prepared to cite occasions where this has caused a particular problem. That way he will be in no doubt as to what is meant. At the end of the day it is hoped the subordinate will recognise and agree the problem areas that need tackling, and you should have raised them in such a way that they are not considered insurmountable barriers to effective work performance, but something which can be overcome jointly.

All this frank and open discussion about an employee's weaknesses should always be balanced with plenty of praise and recognition for work well done. Many managers take the view that "Oh, I don't need to go round patting my staff on the back all day, they know how much I appreciate what a good job they do". In practice, the workforce often does not see it like that and feels that its hard work goes unrecognised. The appraisal interview is at least one occasion on which the record can be put straight.

## Where do We go from Here?

Once some sort of consensus has been reached as to the employee's weaknesses, the next step should be discussion about where improvement is possible and how.

It would be most unfair at this point to tell the employee to go and do something about these problem areas without giving him some idea where to start. At least if he has recognised the problems and accepted the assessment of his work for himself he will be more motivated to find solutions. To get even more co-operation from him the best thing to do is ask him for any ideas he might have as to what might help. He may not come up with many proposals but they can be added to by your own suggestions so that the exercise can be seen as a combined effort.

Some possible solutions may include particular attention to certain tasks, reorganisation of job responsibilities, on-the-job training, a training course, more work experience in a particular area, closer supervision and advice, a college course, further discussion sessions to help deal with particular situations or greater delegation. The employee's failings must have been discussed fairly, and the blame apportioned elsewhere when due or even shared by you. In this way, if the key to improvement is in someone else's hands, this is recognised and can be dealt with without all the burden resting unfairly on the shoulders of the employee under appraisal.

The commitment to improvement must be jointly shared: the employee must have confidence in the proposed solution, and you must show your conviction in the subordinate's ability to reach the necessary standard.

## Summing Up

This is the stage at which all the various parts of the interview can and should be drawn together. You may decide that a lot of time has been spent discussing problems and that you want to redress the balance a bit. This is your opportunity for doing so, since you can use it to re-emphasise the employee's strong points. A general rule of thumb is for the interview to finish on a good note, or at least a positive one of confidence in the employee. If you feel it would be misleading to leave the session on a high note – since the overall appraisal has been pretty poor – it should at least end positively and encouragingly, otherwise any agreed steps towards improvements are not likely to come to much.

There should be a recap on the jointly identified problems, agreed solutions and development plans. This might include adding such details as time-scales, who will do what and dates. Also, if this has not already been covered, you should be trying to find out the employee's hopes and plans for the future. You can then compare them with your own thoughts on the subject and, in the light of everything that has just been discussed, assess how realistic they are and how or whether they might be brought to fruition.

The date of the next formal appraisal should be set, or at least some idea given of when it will be. If more frequent informal meetings are to take place meanwhile, their timing and frequency should also be agreed and finalised.

## A Written Record

At some stage, either during or immediately after the interview, you should make notes on what has taken place. Ideally, only brief notes should be made while the interview is in progress, otherwise it can be very offputting for the employee. They can always be filled out in more detail afterwards. Even if the meeting was only brief, the only way to be sure that nothing important has been missed or forgotten is to write it down. These notes will at least provide basic documentation for next year's appraisal.

Some companies use a special form. Obviously this can have advantages, e.g. when appraisals are used as a basis of comparison between or within departments, since the information will have been recorded in a standardised way. For many managers it provides a useful guide during the interview; they can use it to check that they have covered all the major points and not missed something important. Similarly, it can be used by manager and employee alike prior to the interview; completing it may clarify their thoughts. In that case, a form to be kept on file may be completed at the end of the interview consolidating the views of both parties and incorporating what has been discussed and agreed.

For those who prefer a standard form to the blank-sheet-of-paper approach it should include space for the following information:
- the key areas of the job;
- the strengths and weaknesses of the job-holder;
- suitability for promotion;
- training requirements – now and in the future;
- an overall summary of performance; and
- details of any action plan agreed with the employee.

What happens to such a form, or any report on what happened at the appraisal interview, is often a bone of contention. The question of whether or not it should be shown to the employee is one which can arouse strong views on either side. However, on the basis that the aim of the appraisal is to get joint commitment, and in order to allay suspicions about appraisals, there are good reasons for allowing the employee to see it, to add any comments and possibly to countersign it. A copy of the form should then be retained by you so that you can use it to monitor the action plan, ensure that the necessary help is forthcoming and that the training needs identified are fulfilled. It will then, of course, be part of the necessary documentation for use in next year's appraisal.

## Pitfalls and Problems

The only sure way to achieve effective appraisal interviews is practical experience, but it is at least possible to go into them forewarned about the main pitfalls. These include:

● preparing the official appraisal form before the interview: the employee will feel the whole thing has been prejudged;

● not explaining the purpose of appraisal and the interview;

● asking too many of the wrong type of questions:
  - closed questions,    which make the interview sound like an interrogation;
  - leading questions,    which say too much about the interviewer's own point of view;
  - multiple questions,    which allow the employee only to answer the parts which suit him best;

● ducking the issue whether as a result of the interviewer's failure to tackle the real issues or acceptance of implausible excuses from the employee: this will lose the subordinate's respect and fail to resolve the problem;

● not listening, and talking too much;

● storing up all the criticism of an employee's performance until his once or twice-yearly formal appraisal;

● ridiculing or humiliating the employee, or criticising him for incapabilities he can do nothing about;

● arguing over differences of opinion or controversial points; an appraisal interview should never be allowed to degenerate into an argument;

● allowing the appraisal to drift into a grievance or disciplinary interview;

● making promises or giving undertakings about the future in respect of promotion, training, etc. – without the authority to do so.

## Tactics

Most of these potential difficulties can be overcome with practice and some of the following tactics may help:

● carry out the necessary preparation (see above);

- ask open questions such as:
  - what was the most interesting part of your work this year?
  - what aspects of your work could be improved? How?
  - how do you think you handled . . . ? (state a precise situation)
  - where do you see yourself in two or three years' time?
- get to the point and use specific examples so that the employee can be in no doubt as to which aspect of his performance you mean, and what you want of him;
- agree an action plan for the future; don't leave the employee feeling that all the emphasis has been on his past performance at the expense of future developments;
- keep employees informed on a regular basis of both their strong and their weak points, so that what is said at the appraisal interview will never come as a bolt from the blue;
- give credit for improvement where it is due and recognise the employee's strengths;

## Follow Up and Feedback

Of course, appraisal does not come to an end when the interview does. Whatever joint decisions were reached in the interview will need to be put into action and that will probably involve both the employee and the manager, but particularly the latter. Of course, the other half of your role is to monitor the employee himself. His progress and performance should be checked to see if the action plan is working, and giving the employee feedback on the whole thing is an important method of maintaining his commitment and motivation.

# Disciplinary Interviews

The disciplinary interview is one that most managers and supervisors find difficult: it can be almost as stressful for the interviewer as for the interviewee. However, the ability to conduct such an interview effectively is essential if managers are to do their job properly. To duck out of the process and let misconduct go unchecked will lead to loss of respect from subordinates and to problems from more senior managers who will eventually discover what is going on. This is not to say that managers should act like autocratic martinets; however, if disciplinary problems are tackled at an early stage a great deal of ill-will can be avoided and other employees, hopefully, will see that the organisation does act fairly towards its employees by helping them to attain their previously good standards, rather than letting the matter drift until dismissal is inevitable.

Having said this, though, it is important to stress that you should take only the action provided for in your own company's procedure. Never exceed your brief by carrying out disciplinary interviews if these are the prerogative of more senior managers.

This, perhaps, is the key to effective disciplinary interviews: they should be seen as problem-solving exercises rather than part of a ritual designed to get erring employees out of the door as quickly as possible.

## The Legal Aspects

Disciplinary interviews should not be viewed in a 'legal' context, but it must be accepted that there are three areas of law which do have a bearing on disciplinary matters:

- there is a requirement that all employees who work for 16 hours or more a week be given, within 13 weeks of joining the company, a statement of terms

and conditions of employment including any
disciplinary rules that apply to them;

- employees who have sufficient qualifying service to
claim unfair dismissal (currently two years*), and who
are dismissed for misconduct, must have been treated
reasonably in all the circumstances; which means

- in general terms, that the recommendations contained
in the Code of Practice on disciplinary practice and
procedures, published by the Advisory Conciliation
and Arbitration Service, should have been followed.

## The Code of Practice

The Code stresses that disciplinary procedures should
not be viewed primarily as a means of imposing
sanctions. They should also be designed to emphasise
and encourage improvement in individual conduct.

For the purposes of this chapter its most important
features are as follows:

- the level of management which has authority to take
various forms of disciplinary action should be
specified, but immediate superiors should not
normally have the power to dismiss without reference
to senior management;

- individuals should be informed of the complaints
made against them and should be given the right to
state their case before any disciplinary decisions are
reached;

- employees should have the right to be accompanied
by their trade union representative (when the
organisation recognises a trade union) or a fellow
employee of their choice. However, some thought
must be given to the role of such 'accompanying
people' in your organisation's procedure: for
instance, do they have the right to represent the
employee, or merely to sit by and lend silent moral
support? It is important that both you and they are

---

* For employees whose employment commenced on or after 1.6.85. For
people whose employment began before that date it was one year.

clear about their role before the meeting begins;

● except in special cases, employees should not be dismissed for a first breach of the rules. Exceptions include gross misconduct (e.g. fighting) or cases where breaking the rules could have disastrous consequences – for instance, smoking in an area where highly inflammable materials are stored and where smoking is strictly prohibited;

● no disciplinary action should be taken before a thorough investigation is carried out. Even where it seems that an employee has been caught red-handed, there may be an innocent explanation or it may be that the employee was under the influence of prescribed drugs and so was not aware of what he was doing;

● employees should be given an explanation for any penalty that is imposed; and

● a right of appeal should be given against serious disciplinary action and employees should be told of the procedure for making the appeal.

The Code also considers the problems that may arise if disciplinary action has to be taken against shop stewards. The main point here is that this may be seen as an attack on the union itself. To prevent this occurring the Code recommends that, before any disciplinary action is taken, the matter should be discussed with the convenor or a full-time union official.

## Preparing for the Interview

Perhaps the most important part of preparation for an effective disciplinary interview is the gathering together of the 'evidence'. What do you have to support the allegations of misconduct? Where lateness or absenteeism is concerned, you will obviously need to have the employee's own records, but also check on absence/lateness statistics for other people in the department so that you can support your view that the employee does have a record which is significantly worse than that of others. It is not unknown for one person to be picked on just because his job makes him more visible than other employees.

Where performance standards are concerned, again it should not be too difficult to gather together statistical evidence. Unfortunately, though, disciplinary problems are often not so clear cut. It may be a question of complaints from other employees or even from people outside the company: customers, suppliers, the police, and so on. In such cases it is important that a written record of allegations is compiled and agreed by whoever is making the complaint.

This stage of preparation should never be neglected, even if the employee appears to have been caught red-handed. There may be reasons for the behaviour and, if these can be established during the preparatory stages, so much the better for everybody.

It has to be recognised that, in many cases, you will not be able to provide hard evidence against the employee, but this is not a reason for abandoning the disciplinary process: on the contrary, it makes the disciplinary interview even more important, since it is then that you will have the opportunity to judge the employee's reactions to the allegations.

Another important preparatory stage is to establish, as precisely as possible, exactly what the company rules and procedure provide for similar offences. This does not only mean checking with formal policy documents, though. Have there been similar cases, which may be cited as precedents? How were they dealt with? Why? Were there any special factors?

## Calling the Meeting

Having armed yourself with all relevant information, what of the disciplinary interview itself? The first rule is – do not rush into it! If you do, you will be unprepared but the employee will be even more so. There may be no reasonable possibility for him to account for himself satisfactorily if he is summoned to a meeting out of the blue and faced with allegations which may be extremely serious.

On the other hand, it is of course vital that employees should not be lulled into a false sense of security about any alleged wrong doing.

At the stage when you decide that a disciplinary meeting is necessary, the employee should be alerted to this and given some notice of the date, time and – if this is necessary – the nature of the allegations which will be made. Some notice of the meeting will usually be necessary for your own purposes anyway, so that you can arrange to have a quiet room with no disturbances, and so that the attendance of other people can be organised.

As mentioned above, employees should be invited to bring along a fellow employee of their choice. It is also wise for managers or supervisors to be accompanied – perhaps by a member of the personnel department – since this person can fill two very useful roles:

- taking notes of the meeting; and
- if necessary, ensuring that the discussion does not go off at a tangent by steering the conversation back to the central issue.

However, the extent to which this will be necessary depends on how formal the interview is to be. As a rule of thumb, the more serious the disciplinary action that could result, the more formal the interview should be. At the very early stages, where it is only necessary to tell the employee that, unless he mends his ways, the formal disciplinary procedure will come into play, it is probably best for this to be done on a one to one basis (although this has to be done with care – see page 54). As with all other interviews, an important aspect of the interview is timing: if the disciplinary meeting is likely to provoke a strong reaction – emotional, aggressive, etc. – try to arrange for it to be held at the end of the day or shift, perhaps even at the end of the week. Do remember, though, that it may be necessary to call witnesses in during the interview, so ensure that they will be available.

Where two or more people are alleged to be involved in a disciplinary incident it is usually better to see them separately, ensuring that they are kept apart between the interviews to avoid the possibility of collusion.

## During the Interview

The first point to make about the disciplinary interview is that its tone must be set from the outset. You may be about to make serious charges against someone you know well and with whom you enjoy a good relationship. In this case it is important to distance yourself: to make it clear that you have your 'managerial hat' on; you are speaking about a serious matter as a manager and not as a friend.

However, you should not conduct the meeting as if the employee was already convicted! In many cases, the first concern should be to check if it really is a disciplinary problem. In the case of poor performance, for instance, it may well be that the employee is unable to do the work and requires further training or extra supervision for a period. In the case of absenteeism or poor timekeeping, there may be an underlying domestic problem. If so, counselling is far more appropriate than a disciplinary interview (see page 65).

If you know that it is a disciplinary problem, the employee must be informed clearly of the nature of the allegations made against him, so that he has full opportunity to give his side of the story. If there is fairly lengthy documentation involved which the employee has not had a chance to see previously, e.g. a long letter of complaint from a customer, it will usually be advisable to adjourn the meeting so he can read it properly and then have time to put his thoughts into order before he replies.

If he does dispute the evidence of witnesses, it may be necessary to call them into the meeting, so that they can repeat their evidence and, by listening to – and watching – both of them, you are in a better position to decide who is telling the truth. However, if this is not possible, perhaps because the evidence was provided by a customer who does not want to become involved, it is important to make a note of what the employee has to say, adjourn the meeting and go back to the customer to give the employee's version of events.

## No Conclusive Evidence?

There will be some occasions when it is impossible, at the end of the day, to establish beyond all doubt who is telling the truth. This is where managerial discretion comes into play. Who is most likely to be telling the truth? Consider their previous records, their general attitudes and, importantly, whether the 'accuser' could have a motive for making false allegations. If, having weighed all the pros and cons, you come to the conclusion that the employee did commit an act of misconduct, the absence of conclusive proof should not deter you from continuing with the disciplinary procedure. If a disciplinary matter eventually results in dismissal and an industrial tribunal claim that the dismissal was unfair, the standard of proof required by the tribunal is: was there a genuine belief that the employee had committed the misconduct and was that belief reasonable in all the circumstances?

## Misconduct Admitted

Even if the employee does admit to the misconduct, this is far from the end of the matter. Why did he do it? Were there any mitigating factors? Was he provoked? It is your job to find the answers to these questions, and you can do this best by asking probing questions and showing that you really do want to know the answers: you have the desire, the time, the patience to listen to the answers and to follow them through and evaluate them. If you decide that in view of the employee's answers his behaviour can be excused, the interview can be closed: the employee should be told that the matter is at an end. If not, again the employee has to be told and plans made for the future (see below).

## At the Second Stage

If the disciplinary interview constitutes the second stage of your procedure, it should be conducted along the following lines.
1. Recap on the previous interview, restating the problem and the agreed plan of action.
2. Ask the employee why the agreed improvement has

not transpired. Try to discover whether it is because of events outside his control – machine breakdown, for instance.

3. If outside factors are blamed, adjourn the meeting if necessary while you check out the story.
4. See if there are any mitigating factors.
5. Tell the employee what will happen next (e.g. final written warning) and explain the appeals procedure (see page 55).

**Your own Attitude**

One of the crucial factors in determining the effectiveness of the interview will be your own attitude. Employees who are called in to disciplinary meetings are likely to be nervous, worried, afraid, aggressive or a combination of all four of these. You will have to keep calm, stay in control, handle any common problems as they arise, be reasonable and be objective. A section on handling the most common problems which arise in disciplinary interviews is included on page 52.

# Looking to the Future

Having established your views as to whether the employee did commit the misconduct and having taken account of any mitigating factors, the next step is to plan for the future. As was said at the beginning of this chapter, the interview should be seen in a positive light – as a way of resolving the problem to mutual benefit, not as a necessary prelude to a 'fair' dismissal.

The aim is to get the employee's commitment to agree a course of action which will help to resolve the problem and establish a period of time over which the required improvement(s) will be made. The employee should be warned clearly of the outcome if he fails to improve – final written warning, dismissal, etc. – and all these points should be confirmed to him in writing – either just in the form of a note in the case of minor acts of misconduct or, in more serious cases, in a written warning. The warning should, in essence, summarise the meeting: it should specify the problem; set out the employee's reasons/defences/excuses; state why these have not been accepted (if this is the case); spell out the standards to be attained and any time limits that apply and, finally, warn the employee of the outcome if there is no (or insufficient) improvement.

**Time Limits**

If the employee has been given a time limit of, say, three months in which to demonstrate the required improvement, it is important that, in general, no further formal disciplinary action is taken until the end of that period unless, of course, the employee shows that he has no intention at all of heeding the warning. Of course, this does not mean that you can sit back and forget about the problem until then. Regular review meetings should be held so that the employee's progress can be monitored and any problems dealt with promptly.

If, at the end of the time limit, some improvement has been shown but the employee still has not reached the agreed target, the period may be further extended.

# Gross Misconduct

Cases of extremely serious breaches of the rules such as theft, fighting, assault, drunkenness and so on are referred to as gross misconduct and are usually dealt with by summary dismissal – that is, dismissal with no notice and no pay in lieu of notice. This is often referred to as 'instant dismissal', but there is danger in this terminology. Dismissals should never be instant: they should all be preceded by a thorough investigation and an interview.

**Suspension from Work**

As previously emphasised, interviews should take place after a full investigation, which may take some time. As gross misconduct means that an employee has broken a fundamentally important term of his contract – so important that no reasonable employer could be expected to tolerate his continued employment – this could cause problems in justifying summary dismissal if the employee were allowed to continue to work while the investigation was carried on. Similarly, you cannot allow somebody who is clearly drunk to operate machinery, nor can you risk allowing participants in a fight to remain together.

The answer in all these cases is to suspend the employees concerned, on full pay, until the disciplinary interview can be convened. It is important to stress that the suspension must not result in loss of earnings. If it does it carries a strong presumption that they have been judged to be guilty right from the start and, since such action would be in breach of their contract, it could lead to a claim for damages being made against the company in the County Court.

The employees should be informed that the disciplinary procedure is to be invoked, that they may be summarily dismissed, and they will be notified of the time and date of the disciplinary interview in sufficient time for them to arrange to be accompanied by a fellow worker or union representative.

**Misconduct Outside Work**

In general terms, what employees do in their own time and away from work is a matter for them alone and has nothing to do with their employer. As with all general rules, though, there are exceptions. Examples include:

● people in a position of trust who are found guilty of offences concerning dishonesty;

● employees who can only perform their job effectively if their reputation in the local community is of good standing; and

● employees such as drivers who lose their driving licence for a substantial period.

In these cases, too, no action should be taken without prior investigation and interview.

**Involvement of Police**

The involvement of the police in gross misconduct cases can cause enormous problems for managers trying to conduct disciplinary meetings. One of the main difficulties which arises is when employees refuse to participate in the meeting in case it prejudices a forthcoming trial. The ideal solution in such an instance is to suspend the employee on full pay pending the outcome of the criminal proceedings, making it clear to the employee that a senior manager will attend the trial and the employee will then be invited to attend a disciplinary meeting at which his future with the company will be decided – always assuming the employee is not then languishing in prison!

It is important, though, to stress to the employee that the outcome of the trial will not automatically determine the outcome of the disciplinary hearing. The burden of proof will be quite different, as will the factors to be taken into account by the court on the one hand and the company on the other.

However, although this procedure represents the ideal, it is not always practicable. It may take months for the case to come to court and the company may well take the view that it cannot afford to wait that long, or it may decide that there is already enough evidence available for it to proceed with the disciplinary meeting. In this case, it may be wise to allow the employee to be accompanied by his solicitor so that he does not incriminate himself inadvertently. If this is allowed, it should be made quite clear to the solicitor that he is only there to hold a watching brief: while he may warn his client off certain areas, he may not represent him during the meeting.

If the employee refuses to attend the meeting even on these conditions, he should be warned that he will be denying himself the opportunity of explaining his action or of putting forward any mitigating factors and that the company will have to go ahead and make its decision on whether or not to dismiss in the absence of this information.

If the employee is remanded in custody and so is unable to attend the interview, it is a good idea to contact his solicitor and ask him along to the meeting to speak for his client.

The one course that should never be taken is to hold the interview in the presence of the police. This effectively deprives people of the right to state their case since, quite often, there may be points they could make in their own favour as far as the company is concerned but which might be highly prejudicial as far as the police are concerned. It is very important that disciplinary and legal proceedings are kept quite separate.

Equally, you should never dismiss solely on the basis of a confession made to the police: there have been cases in the past when the courts have accepted that confessions have been made under duress.

## The Problem Areas

The one thing you can rely on with disciplinary meetings is that they will not all go smoothly. All sorts of problems will arise and it is important to be aware of the more common ones so that you are prepared to deal with them if and when they arise.

### Walking Out of the Meeting

Occasionally, when faced with allegations that they believe to be totally unjustified – or perhaps because they are furious at being found out – some employees lose their temper and try to storm out of the meeting. Above all else, if this happens, you have to stay calm. Your tactics will have to depend on your assessment of why the employee is behaving in that way: is it because he is genuinely overwrought, or is he trying to make you give up the disciplinary meeting? If you think he is genuinely out of control, it may be sensible to tell him that you are going to adjourn the meeting – for half an hour or possibly even until the next day – so that he can calm down, but then the interview will resume.

In other cases, inform the employee that his behaviour is verging on gross misconduct: unless he is prepared to allow the meeting to continue, you will have to take the matter to a higher level of management and dismissal may result.

Similarly, if the employee starts to argue during the meeting, you must make it clear that you are not interested in an argument: the purpose of the meeting is to try to identify the problem and resolve it – for that his co-operation is necessary. Arguing will only damage his position. Try to explain the difference between a rational discussion and shouting the same thing over and over again!

Another variation on this theme is the employee who bursts into tears during the interview. Again, you have to decide whether this is genuine emotion or merely a ploy to try to avoid disciplinary action being taken, and deal with it accordingly: offer a cup of tea, or perhaps an adjournment, but make it clear that the interview will continue.

## Disruption in the Workplace

Other employees might behave with apparent calmness during the meeting, but then return to their workplace and cause considerable disruption: there have been cases of people who have slammed out of their manager's office after being given a written warning, torn the warning up into small pieces, thrown them on to the floor, and jumped up and down on them while shouting obscenities about their boss! Other cases are somewhat less dramatic, but may have a more insidious effect when they involve the employee disrupting others in the workplace by enlisting their aid and sympathy against the wicked management!

In all these sorts of incident, some allowance has to be made for the fact that the employees are acting under stress and, perhaps, are behaving right out of character. It may be best if they are sent home and asked to return next morning to give an assurance that they will cease their disruptive behaviour and work normally.

## Counselling to Discipline

A problem to beware of is the informal discipline/counselling meeting which turns gradually into a disciplinary interview, without this being planned. Take, for instance, the situation where you become aware that standards seem to be slipping generally. You decide that you will 'have a word' with the key people in the department to try to establish what is going wrong, and one of these people becomes very defensive, will not answer your questions fully, or leads you to believe that he is deliberately slacking.

In such a situation, it is very important that you recognise the point when it becomes a disciplinary matter, as you must then adjourn the meeting so that you can carry out the necessary preliminaries; in particular, so that the employee can have the opportunity to be accompanied by a fellow worker of his choice. In one recent case a fairly routine meeting developed into a disciplinary meeting which resulted in the employee resigning. He successfully claimed constructive (unfair) dismissal because the tribunal felt that a disciplinary meeting in the presence of two senior managers, when the employee had no opportunity to have somebody to accompany him, put undue pressure on him.

## No Representative Present

There may be cases where an employee refuses to accept an invitation to be accompanied by a union representative or co-worker. This should not present a real problem: many employees who get into trouble at work would rather none of their colleagues knew of the problem; others may have mitigating factors to put forward which they would be embarrassed to let other employees know about, such as illness or domestic problems. If you feel it is essential that someone else is there to act as a witness, perhaps someone from the personnel department could be present.

## New Employees

Unless it is expressly provided for in the employment contract, employees who do not have the necessary qualifying service to claim unfair dismissal do not necessarily have to be treated in accordance with the disciplinary procedure if they break company rules. However, it may well be very sensible to go through the procedure, at least in its early stages. New employees who have come from a totally different sort of company, or who have come straight from school, may well turn into model employees after an encounter with your disciplinary procedure. Merely firing them and replacing them with new people – who may well turn out to be even less satisfactory – is very expensive and will do nothing for the company's image, nor for its labour relations.

## Appeals Procedures

The ACAS Code of Practice on Disciplinary Practice and Procedures at Work (see page 42) says that, whilst grievance procedures are sometimes used for dealing with disciplinary appeals, it is normally more appropriate to keep the two kinds of procedure separate since disciplinary issues are in general best resolved within the organisation and need to be dealt with more speedily than others.

All statements of terms and conditions of employment should include a note specifying the person to whom employees can apply if they are dissatisfied with any disciplinary decisions, but it is sensible to remind employees of the procedure whenever formal disciplinary action is taken against them. After all, how many of your employees will remember having been given their statements, let alone know what they said? It must be remembered that it is much better for any mistake in procedure – or any mitigating factors – to be revealed in an internal procedure rather than to surface during an industrial tribunal hearing.

In particular, employees who have had disciplinary action taken against them should be told:

● to whom they should address their appeal;
● whether there are any time limits within which the appeal must be lodged;
● whether or not they have to give the grounds of their appeal;
● whether the disciplinary action will be suspended pending the outcome of the appeal.

Ideally, appeals should be directed to a level of management one stage higher than that involved in the disciplinary decision. This, though, is not always possible. In some organisations it is only the top level of management which can take disciplinary decisions. In this case, there are three possible options:

- an appeal can be made to the manager who took the original decision;
- no right of appeal may be given; or
- there can be a right of appeal to an independent arbitrator – ACAS keep a list of people who are prepared to act in this capacity.

In general, the first option is preferable, since it does provide an opportunity for the employee to supply new, relevant information and for the company to review the procedure it has adopted. The third option, while it might seem to be the fairest, does pose problems. Careful thought has to be given before passing disciplinary decisions – particularly those on dismissal – to outside third parties. Also, there will be a temptation for the arbitrator to try to find a compromise. In the case of an employee appealing against dismissal, there really cannot be a sensible middle way: either he is dismissed or he is reinstated!

# Grievance Interviews

Many managers or supervisors would find it difficult to identify situations that are formal grievance interviews. They handle complaints, requests and queries from their staff on an informal basis every day. However, this informal activity is also supplemented in most companies by a formal grievance procedure and, in some cases, by a disputes procedure agreed with a recognised trade union to cover collective grievances.

## Individual Grievances

The law requires an employer to specify in an employee's written terms and conditions of employment a person to whom a grievance concerning employment can be addressed. This should also: specify the manner, e.g. oral or written, in which such a grievance should be raised; and, where the grievance procedure is taken in steps, explain them, or if these details are contained in any other document, it should be made reasonably accessible to employees.

The Industrial Relations Code of Practice says that grievance procedures should be designed to settle the grievance fairly and as near as possible to the point of origin. They should be simple, rapid and, of course, in writing.

### Example Procedure

"The Company's policy is to encourage free interchange and communication between managers and the staff they manage. This ensures that questions and problems can be aired and resolved quickly.

1. If you have a grievance arising out of your employment you should raise the matter with your immediate superior in the first instance. If the matter is not resolved after five working days, you may put your grievance, in writing, to your Departmental Manager.

2. If the matter remains unresolved at this level after five working days you may request that the matter is referred for the decision of the appropriate Director, whose decision is final.

3. You may consider some requests or complaints too personal to discuss with your immediate Supervisor or Manager. With these matters you have the right to go to the Personnel Manager after first receiving permission from your Manager or Supervisor to do so.

We wish to ensure that any employee problem or grievance is dealt with effectively and speedily. Your co-operation is sought in bringing such matters to your Supervisor's or Manager's attention as they arise."

## Disputes Procedure

Some types of grievance, over pay for example, are raised as an individual grievance but may affect many other employees as well. Where there is no union presence in a company the same procedure will normally be used to deal with grievances of a collective nature. Where there is a separate collective procedure the manager or supervisor would be sensible to identify the nature of the grievance as early as possible and select the correct procedure in order to process it effectively.

In companies where trade unions are recognised, a separate collective disputes procedure will usually exist. This procedure is meant to deal with:

● disputes over the interpretation or application of existing agreements or the terms and conditions under which employees are employed; and

● disputes which relate to either the management or employees (the union) wishing to propose changes to those agreements or terms and conditions of employment.

Once again, the Code of Practice suggests that such procedures should be in writing, state the level at which the issue should first be raised, and lay down time limits for each procedural step with a provision for extension by agreement. It is also usual for such agreements to preclude strikes or lock outs or any other form of industrial action until all stages of the procedure have been completed and a failure to agree is formally recorded.

In both types of grievance procedure there is often provision for employees to be accompanied by a colleague or trade union representative if they so wish.

## The Need to Listen to Grievances

As already noted, grievances are taken as part of the day to day management of employees and the way that grievances are heard is usually very informal. Whatever the degree of formality, there are some useful hints which can make these encounters successful in resolving workplace problems. After all, if employees cannot vent their feelings and have things properly explained to them, resentment may well escalate into major conflicts, or employees who are valuable to the business may leave and go elsewhere if the atmosphere is intolerable.

There is one problem with grievances: some managers holding positions of authority do not like to have grievances presented to them. They react defensively perhaps seeing them as a personal attack, or a waste of valuable management time which could be better spent doing other things. However, stifling employees from taking grievances by this angry, negative response deprives managers of very valuable feed-back. Even if it is a falsely based grievance, hearing out the matter will ensure that misconceptions are corrected, not only for the employee who brought it, but also for other colleagues who are labouring under these illusions.

Never forget that even a false grievance may be hiding a real problem which can be uncovered during the course of a grievance interview if you are prepared to probe a little. Someone with a personal problem may use a 'pretend' grievance in order to get your attention. The real secret of handling grievance interviews, whether they are informal or formal, is to respond by welcoming the grievance; give it proper attention, treat it seriously and, of course, listen very carefully.

As with any kind of interview, try to ensure that the employee is taken aside to an office or place where there will be no interruption. Make sure that seats are available and it is a reasonably comfortable environment.

Taking the employee away from the work area is also a sensible precaution, in some cases, to stop other employees joining in and turning the interview into a general harangue that could get quite out of control.

## How to Structure the Interview

You should aim to establish precisely what the grievance is about without airing your own views about the topic. If the employees are angry it would be almost impossible to stem the torrent anyway. Great self-control is required of the interviewer; once the employees have run out of steam it is possible to establish what they are complaining about.

Managers usually view things from a different perspective from that of their subordinates. For instance, Joe Smith might have brought a grievance about not wanting to work voluntary overtime to his immediate supervisor, who then reports it to his boss as "Joe Smith wants to see you about a grievance and he is refusing to be instructed by me".

When the boss interviews Joe Smith it becomes apparent that the real source of the grievance was the manner in which the request to work overtime was made. In every other respect Joe Smith is quite willing to do the extra time.

So, once the object of the grievance is clearly understood, the manager will want to know what the employee's point of view is – to allow him to state his case. Why does he feel the way he does; persuade him to give examples and provide further information if he can. Usually employees are fairly inarticulate or apprehensive about questioning authority, so often you will have to ask questions to clarify the situation and provide additional information.

It is far better to keep the detailed questioning until

after the employee has stated his case because, if interrupted, the employee will frequently lose the thread of the argument. It is quite usual for people in this situation to say "I'm not very good at explaining" or "Do you see what I mean?" or some such thing. It is a concealed plea for assistance which allows you to summarise what has been understood of the employee's case so far.

State factually what has been understood, but it is also very useful to include the emotional overtones of the employee's case, e.g. "So, Joe, you are angry at the supervisor pushing the rota list under your nose and ordering you to sign it". There should be no indication from the interviewer that he approves or disapproves, is sympathetic or condones the views given by the employee.

There is usually little point at this stage in getting the employee to look dispassionately and objectively at the problem. Nor is it very effective to meet complaints with counter-complaints, which is a common response of the manager who feels under attack. Very often it is necessary to investigate the grievance by speaking to other parties involved before continuing the interview.

If they are not carefully handled, grievance interviews can have two pitfalls:

- employees, acting in the heat of the moment, can provide examples of the sort of behaviour that can get them sacked for gross misconduct; and

- managers acting defensively who, rightly or wrongly, turn the grievance interview into a disciplinary matter.

If either of these two situations arises it would be wise to suspend the employees on full pay (or without if the contract of employment allows) and call them back to a redefined meeting – a disciplinary meeting. The issues should be clearly stated beforehand, perhaps in a letter confirming the suspension and recalling the employees to the premises.

### Explaining the Management Position

Once the emotional temperature has cooled it will be

possible to explain the management position. This means giving a clear explanation of the reasons that caused decisions to be made or situations to happen. For instance "Joe, your supervisor has told me that he was extremely pushed for time and was hurrying to get to a meeting. His manner was abrupt but the way he put the rota list before you reflected his anxiety to get away for the meeting". Other explanations of the company's position might include company policy and rules, collective agreements or administrative procedures, depending on the nature of the grievance.

At this stage you should invite the employee to ask clarifying questions and to show that the management's position is understood, even though the employee may be a long way from accepting it.

In the process of discussing the grievance a lot of common ground will be revealed and, equally, the main points of disagreement will be highlighted. Suggestions can then be made by either side as to how the disagreement can be resolved. In most cases there is scope for modification although sometimes a manager will have to say that he considers the grievance to be without foundation and no action will be taken.

## Deciding What to Do

Deciding what to do is the manager's prerogative but it is vital that you do not agree to a course of action that is beyond your level of authority and so may be countermanded by more senior managers. Very often discussions about what can be done will include explaining the constraints that you must work under, e.g. whether you have the power to authorise a transfer or cash refund, etc. However, these constraints should not be allowed to justify doing nothing if there is merit in the case. Perhaps you can represent the case to a more senior manager who has the power to modify the rules. In the case of Joe, an apology from his supervisor might seem the best tactic but there might be some background history that makes this impossible. Certainly they should be brought face to face in your presence, so that there is an opportunity to patch things up.

In more serious situations, where a subordinate employee appears to have a well-founded grievance, it may be necessary to refer it to a higher level where there is the necessary authority to put the situation to rights. This is especially tricky because there must always be some form of face saving for the supervisor or manager concerned.

If a complaint is made against another member of staff there is a natural tendency to keep such a matter as confidential as possible – not even the person about whom the complaint is made may be told. However it is usually essential to know both sides of the story and so this really is not a practicable approach. It is far better to involve the other person and treat the matter openly. The decision that is made must be fair to both parties and if the person only hears about the complaint through the grapevine he might jump to the conclusion that he has been treated badly.

It may be sensible to adjourn grievance interviews pending discussions with other managers or to seek further advice, which would also give time for the employee to reflect on the discussions. Sheer procrastination should be avoided but a lapse of time before the decision is made at least shows that the decision is not an instant, 'off the top of your head' reaction. Sometimes it is a good idea to think aloud to test the employee's reaction to a decision which is likely to go against him: "I don't know quite what to decide yet, but I think I shall have to disappoint you unless my manager has any views about changing the rules".

It has to be accepted that some grievances cannot be resolved in the way the employee would wish. It only remains in such cases to explain to the employee the decision that has been taken regarding the grievance, including the reasons for that decision. It might be sensible to confirm the conversation in writing, especially if it is likely that the employee will pursue the matter to the next stage of the grievance procedure to a more senior manager or director of the company.

# Follow-up

Whatever decisions are made as a result of the grievance interview it is important that the situation is reviewed. Check the temperature to see if the situation is settling down, if it was decided to take no action. If some form of action was agreed, it is vital to check that the decision is being implemented. There is no grievance like the one apparently redressed but which has not been implemented! It is also worthwhile checking that the changes being carried out actually do have the effect that was intended.

# Counselling Interviews

What is special about counselling? Why do supervisors
and managers need to know about counselling
techniques? Surely, the personnel department ought to
be dealing with all the employees' problems that need
the counselling approach!

This, though, is a dangerous view: counselling is an
important man-management technique which is far too
useful to leave entirely to the personnel profession.
Indeed, some companies are too small to have a
specialist department, or the workplace may be too far
away from centralised service departments.

Traditional managers/supervisors have always been
happiest when they have been diagnosing machinery
faults or sorting out production hiccups: they almost
always shy away from the more delicate personal and
work related problems of their human colleagues. "Send
them round to personnel" is about the most constructive
response you can get, but more likely the whole
situation is ignored.

However, when they eventually do take up the
counselling role, they will find it an effective tool in
improving the usefulness of employees to the company.
It also demonstrates that the 'powers that be' do care.
Counselling can also be used to stimulate commitment
and co-operation amongst employees and provide an
important communication channel for managers and
their subordinates.

In fact, counselling techniques can make managers
and supervisors much more effective in their respective
roles. They must be seen as a fundamental part of the
job of managing people. The need for counselling arises
far more frequently at work than is generally
recognised.

Please do not think that these techniques are only for
use in the workplace; family problems and social
situations involving relationships between people will

also bring these techniques into play. In considering the various aspects of counselling it will soon be clear that these techniques can be used in many work situations; in particular, in the management of teams to maximise the input and involvement of the individuals in that team. One of the most important techniques is something which is apparently simple – listening – and this is something that we could all do better.

## Managing Employees

There are a variety of ways supervisors or line managers can get the work done through the employees they manage. In the main this involves ordering or asking for work to be carried out in a specific way or at a particular time. Persuasion, other inducements or incentives can also be offered to obtain employees' co-operation depending on the specific situation. However, when employees try to carry out the instructions of their supervisors and are frustrated by their failures or they are unable to cope with the personal relationships involved in their work, neither coercion nor persuasion will resolve the problem. This is when counselling can be used with good effect.

Counselling interviews are designed to allow subordinates to gain new perspectives about problems that restrict their usefulness to the company. Ideally they will allow employees to identify the causes of the problems that lie within themselves and which will require a change of attitude and/or behaviour before they are resolved.

Since many of these problems could result in the employee being dismissed, counselling can be seen as a means of solving work problems without wasting human resources.

## What is Counselling?

Counselling is not just a matter of being 'nice to employees': of sitting back passively, dispensing tea and sympathy. Certainly, sympathy and understanding are needed to establish rapport, but counselling calls for managers to put themselves inside the other person's world, to see what things look like from his point of view.

Counselling interviews should not be seen as an opportunity to 'straighten out' employees or to display and enforce the manager's authority. They do not call for managers to devise solutions to the problems and then impose them upon the employees because of genuine paternalistic concern. The solutions to the problem have to come from the individual employees themselves and must have their commitment behind them. The interview must not become an emotional outpouring; it should be a rational discussion of the problems. Neither should it be treated as a social event designed to ease tensions in the department or between manager and subordinate. It goes without saying that it is not an opportunity to 'sell' the employees a solution as an ideal way to get rid of the problem, particularly when the solution might not be in their best interests.

It must be quite apparent by now that managers or supervisors who use counselling techniques will require an attitude which is most unusual for 'leaders' to adopt. Rather than being the people who order things to be done they have to repress their natural instincts to manage and, instead, work on creating the environment in which the solutions can be worked out by the employees concerned. So what sort of skills are required to carry out a counselling interview? In many respects these are ordinary social skills. One researcher, Argyle, has compiled a list of attributes that a manager/counsellor needs to have or to acquire:

● a warm and friendly manner;
● ability to treat the employee as an equal;
● ability to get the conversation going in a smooth, easy way and to maintain it by asking open-ended questions like "why don't you tell me what's on your mind?" or just "tell me about it";
● ability to find some common interest, experience or other bond so that the parties can identify with each other, e.g. supporting the same soccer team, or both having daughters called Anne;
● ability to give full attention and listen carefully to

what the employee has to say; and

● ability to use the employee's own way of speaking, words, conventions, etc; in fact, generally meeting people on their own ground.

The attributes mentioned above create a favourable atmosphere in which to hold the interview. However, the interviewer has responsibility for leading the employee, step by step, towards a resolution. To do this, the positive skills of reflection, clarification, summarising and listening have to be used.

## Preparing the Interview

It is only possible to talk about structuring and planning in the broadest terms. No two counselling interviews are ever the same and flexibility of approach is essential. However, careful tacticians will always ensure that, before calling the interview, the employee's individual file has been checked thoroughly. For instance:

● how old is the employee; what are the personal circumstances;

● how long has the person been employed; check appraisal forms, selection interview reports, etc.;

● are there any indications of outside problems affecting work, e.g. mortgage references, court attendances, etc;

● what information can the person's supervisor or previous supervisor give;

● what is the employee's sickness record like and how much overtime is being worked.

Sometimes, though, when the employee initiates the interview, these precautionary steps are not possible.

It is not uncommon for the problems that are likely to surface at the interview to be quite outside the expertise of the interviewer. Money problems, housing problems and marital difficulties are often areas where specialist help is required. It is extremely helpful to know where to direct the employee for such assistance. Do not try to give advice on subjects that you know nothing about: knowing where the Citizens Advice Bureau is situated, perhaps ensuring the personnel department has an up-to-date book on, say, State benefits, or providing access to other works of reference or useful people who can give advice, will be of far greater help to the employee.

## The Interview Environment

As with any other kind of interview, it is important to ensure that sufficient time is set aside for the encounter. Ensure that interruptions are channelled elsewhere. The constant ringing of the telephone interrupting the discussion will kill the counselling session stone dead. Excluding interruptions will also show the importance that you have placed on the occasion. Ensure that these interviews are arranged in the normal business environment; the pub down the road or the social club will be a distracting venue. Any room that has a comfortable temperature, comfy chairs and reasonable lighting levels will do. Sometimes, pre-arranged coffee or tea will help to lubricate the proceedings.

Try to make sure that the interview is not timed to take place when the employee is under heavy work or time pressures. If a relaxed atmosphere is to be achieved the interview must not be hurried along to a conclusion. The impression should be given that there is ample time to deal with any problems that emerge.

## The Structure of Counselling

Broadly speaking, the interview should fall into three main phases, though it does pay to remember that the counselling interviewer should be sufficiently flexible to deal with the kinds of problem raised:

● at first the employee will need to be encouraged to talk about the problem(s) and you will have to use all the normal pleasantries to set the employee at ease. You must listen carefully, but more about this later. If the employee has requested the meeting then it is important to establish quickly what it is all about. If the interviewer has requested the meeting then the purpose of the meeting should be explained from the outset;

● as the discussion continues, you should try to help

the employee gain a fuller understanding of the problem, e.g. why other employees react badly to brusqueness or to brittle sarcasm; was the employee aware of the effect or simply oblivious of it?

There should be ample discussion of possible solutions and this is where the interviewer can contribute knowledge, experience or just common sense to evaluate the range of possibilities. These solutions should be discussed thoroughly including their advantages, disadvantages and any other implications of deciding to adopt any of the solutions. Some thought should be given to how these solutions might be implemented. The employee must work slowly through the counselling process playing a full part in piecing solutions together and deciding which option to pick up.

The importance of getting on the employee's 'wave-length' cannot be stressed too much. Employees will be willing to be frank and constructive providing the interviewer does not make them feel stupid or unusual because they have a problem. If the interviewer can also put across the belief that a solution can usually be found to human problems or, at the very least, that 'a trouble shared is a trouble halved' progress can be made. However if it also becomes clear that you are bored, cynical, disapproving or just plain stumped, the employee will lose the incentive to confront his problems with your help.

Finally, you should end the interview by summarising the progress made and checking over plans for implementing any decision and, above all, ensuring that another interview is planned to check progress.

From this you can see that it is necessary to keep some notes on the discussions setting out:

(a)    the solutions and aims that have been set by the employee; and

(b)    the methods to be used to achieve the objectives.

**Establishing the Facts**

The discussion can only begin to be fruitful if the

interview is geared towards establishing the facts of the situation. Those magic one word questions: Who? What? Where? Why? When? How? should be milked to the full. Encourage the employee to continue contributing to the discussion by showing, by your listening attitude, that you consider what is being said is important. Try not to be impatient or to cut off the discussion if the employee digresses.

**Counselling Model Diagram**

| Phases | Counselling Interviewer's Role |
|---|---|
| 1. Establishing 'contact'<br><br>Hearing the story and making the facts clear<br><br>Understanding the problem | Putting employees at ease; encouraging them to talk by listening; helping a full understanding of the problem to be gained; and providing specific information |
| 2. Solution and decision making | Talk through likely advantages and disadvantages, bearing in mind what is the best solution for the employee and how can it be put into action. Guide the process of decision-making but employees must make own decisions |
| 3. Plan of campaign and follow-up | Summarise progress made; help create action plan and arrange future follow-up interview(s) |

**Listening**

We all slip into sloppy listening habits from time to

time; we all know when to turn a deaf ear, and when we do not want to hear we can easily achieve that aim. However, counselling managers must listen intelligently.

The main reasons why people are poor listeners are as follows:

● they like the sound of their own voices, preoccupied as they are with their own opinions and ideas. These people concentrate on jumping in at every pause in the other person's conversation with their own viewpoint;

● they know that they are not listening properly but do not know what to do to remedy the situation, especially when understanding has accelerated ahead of the oral communication of the speaker; and

● they simply lack practice at listening.

An important first step in the interview is to ensure you sit up straight, look alert and do not loll about in a chair, allowing yourself to be distracted by outside interruptions. Look at the employee and maintain eye contact. Do not doodle and fold up paper clips in a thousand contortions. Keep an open mind. You may have heard it all before and know all the ins and outs of the employee concerned but there may be some important change of view or fact that comes to light. Try to spot the main aspects of the problem – as the employee sees them.

There are several barriers to intelligent listening. The words that are used may cause confusion, e.g. specialists who have developed their own professional vocabulary may confound the listener; the way something is said can make understanding difficult; and even regional accents can wreak havoc.

However, the counselling manager must realise that these language problems are his responsibility and must be dealt with. Even apparent understanding and active head-nodding can cover a great deal of confusion which can only be determined if the interviewer asks questions to check understanding. The best way is to ask the employee to repeat in his own words what you have just said. The reply will help you to adjust the vocabulary level and general presentation.

72

Sometimes the words get across but the wrong message is interpreted because the employee is too emotionally involved or biased. It would be unwise to accept as fact the reasons for a marriage break-up from one side of the partnership alone. This means that you must question carefully and gain further information before accepting the employee's story as a basis for counselling.

Listening can also be careless. A manager might only listen to the bits that are interesting or confirm beliefs or prejudices. Other, possibly important, parts of the message are shut out. Additionally, the manager might be tempted to anticipate what is going to be said and therefore fail to listen to what actually is said. Another irritating habit is finishing off the employee's sentences or supplying an appropriate (?) word. These are conversation stoppers. The time spent waiting for employees to express themselves can profitably be spent in the following ways:

● studying the way the employee speaks – 'body language' can give many important clues to the genuineness of what is being said;

● listening with the 'third ear' to sense the unspoken meanings, feelings, beliefs and prejudices that may be behind what the employee is saying. This underlying problem has been termed 'the hidden agenda' that employees will not articulate until they see how the manager reacts to the other things that have been said. If they feel that trust has been established and the manager is trying to be helpful rather than censorious the real problem will be brought into the open.

Very often this does not happen until the very end of the interview. The employee may be trying to protect himself from full discussion of the issue while still wanting the counsellor to know of his problem. Consequently, the matter is brought up late in the day when there may be little time for further discussion. Perhaps a further interview can be arranged;

● listening on two levels: train one part of your mind to listen carefully to what is said and the other half to

analyse and judge the ideas being expressed;
● making a quick summary of what the employee has said.

Do not forget, another listening skill is to tolerate and understand the silences. They can mean that employees are embarrassed or irritated but may also mean that employees are about to go forward with new insight into their problems.

## Why Counsel?

At this point a manager might wonder if there are enough hours in the day to cope with counselling interviews and dealing with other people's problems. In practice this need not happen. Time spent like this will often sort out what will become intractable work problems if they are left to fester. The dividing line between work and personal problems can be very narrow.

Many managers like to think that they operate an 'open door' policy. The fact that nobody comes in to discuss personal or job related problems is seen as proof that everyone is happy and coping well. Approachable managers will always be alert for the limits of ordinary conversation and will realise that there are issues that employees would want to raise if given a realistic chance to do so.

### Job-related Counselling

Ordinary day to day discussions can amount to counselling without the manager concerned realising it. For instance, how often do employees come along and say that they have been unable to do a particular job, or that a promotion or transfer has been offered to them and they want your opinion as to whether they should take it? It is quite natural that employees should speak to their boss about such problems and it is the responsibility of the manager to give the help that is needed. The first step, of course, is to establish the facts (even investigate the facts with other involved parties), then talk through the options and, finally, see if a decision can be made and a course of action settled upon. This does not mean that the manager supplies his own solution and then tells the employee what to do to achieve it. This will kill the employee's initiative and will not help to improve his ability to cope with problems. It will make him more dependent rather than help to develop his self-reliance and maturity.

## Counselling Personal Problems

This kind of counselling may result from employees asking their manager for help, or from the manager forcing employees to talk about personal matters that are affecting their performance. Indeed, managers could be a little more alert to counselling opportunities. How many times do employees ask for an advance of wages or a loan which is treated by the manager as a straightforward sanctioning situation with few questions asked and, above all, no great involvement? The employee, when asked, may not wish to discuss the situation and may even resent the intrusion but there will be many who will welcome the opportunity to unburden themselves to a sympathetic listener.

Once again the primary task is fact-finding. Employees must be allowed to ventilate their problems in their own way, however rambling and hesitant this may be. When the employee has talked himself out, you should explain your role in the discussion – "Well I understand what you're saying but there aren't any ready made solutions to your problem. But let us toss it around together and see what happens. From what you are saying the problem amounts to . . ." It is important that the employee realises that you are not going to take over the problem, but only wish to help him to find his own solution. This highlights the counselling techniques of clarification and summarising.

Clarifying remarks do help to illuminate the problem for employees concerned but never comment or make an attack on the employee's self-image, e.g. "It is because you're so immature and emotional that you can't handle it". This is very counter-productive. It is also unwise to show surprise or disapproval, or express value judgements on things that employees have said.

Such responses will make employees turn away from the counselling process.

You should always summarise the situation once the employee has aired his problems. The summary should be put in a non-critical way, so that the employee can agree that it is a true reflection of the situation. This also provides the opportunity for employees to correct misunderstandings and to feel that the interviewer now has a complete grasp of the problem.

## Making Decisions

Since counselling managers cannot control the actual decisions made by the employee, how can they contribute to the decision making process? Sets of ready made alternatives should not be presented to the employee, rather the interviewer should give clues and nudges in the right direction based, perhaps, on an input of knowledge or experience. Such inputs are best phrased as questions, e.g: Do you think the Citizens Advice Bureau could help? Have you seen your doctor about it? Briefly, the interviewer's role is to see that, whatever the decision, it is made on sensible grounds.

Several possible solutions might be in the interviewer's mind but the one adopted by the employee must be appropriate for the kind of person he is. For instance, if security and freedom from debt are overriding considerations, a solution that involves taking out a second mortgage is unlikely to appeal.

Many employees tend to get over-involved in a problem so that they cannot see the wood for the trees or they cling misguidedly to false assumptions. You should work at giving employees an insight or new view of their problems by using clues or calling attention to part of the solution. This way employees can fit together the whole solution and call it their own. This is much more effective than presenting off-the-peg solutions that will not attract their commitment.

It is possible on occasions for the manager to offer very constructive help. For instance, arranging compassionate leave or extended leave of absence to give the employee time to sort out the personal problems. Alcoholics can be given time and treatment to dry out. Hours of work can be temporarily altered so that children can be taken to school when the normal arrangements fall through.

Of course, some problems do not appear to have solutions of a practical kind. Someone who is grieving over the death of a close relative or whose spouse has left home can frequently only be met with genuine sympathy and moral support; indeed, this is all that is usually sought.

It is important for the manager to bear in mind that sympathy for employees should be tempered by the need to keep the work flowing properly. Any special dispensation should be thoroughly discussed with senior managers to ensure that it does not clash with company policy or form a precedent that will cause problems in the future.

## Planning Actions

If the employee decides to take up one of the solutions it is extremely useful to work out an action plan then and there. However, the decision might happen some days later after the employee has had time to reflect on matters and this illustrates the necessity for arranging a follow-up interview at a later date. Any plan of campaign must be organised systematically and should include a timetable that is realistic in the light of the pressures and demands placed on the employee. Continuing support and encouragement might be given informally or by scheduling further meetings to review the state of play.

## How to Learn the Skills

Counselling skills are social skills and are mostly learnt through practice. Why not start right away? When the next employee reports that, for instance, a personal item is lost – listen to the employee's story; establish the facts (was it actually brought to work); ask if he has looked in any particular (named) places; establish that he knows what the procedure is for reporting lost goods or explain where this information can be obtained. Help him achieve a plan of campaign to report or search for the missing item. He may think that you are stark staring mad but you have just conducted your first counselling interview – no doubt, quite successfully.

Sometimes, courses in sensitivity training or counselling skills where there is opportunity for role play can give just the right amount of confidence to managers to start using counselling techniques. A counselling checklist (to be answered truthfully) may help managers monitor their progress in using counselling techniques.

1. Did I put the employee at ease?
2. How did I cope with anxiety or hostility?
3. Did I listen effectively and encourage the employee to talk?
4. Did I see the problem from the employee's point of view?
5. Did I try to understand the employee's silences?
6. Did I go at the employee's own speed?
7. Did I provide relevant factual information at the appropriate time?
8. Did I clarify confused ideas?
9. Did I give the interview a pattern or framework?
10. Did I discuss with the employee what the meeting was intended to achieve and how it would be carried out?
11. Did I impose insights or did I encourage them?
12. Did I avoid unnecessary emotional involvement and treat the problem in a detached, clinical way?
13. Did I give advice that I was qualified to give?
14. Did I not pry unnecessarily into the private life of the employee, his family or friends?

If you repeat this exercise on a regular basis, your confidence in your counselling ability will grow as you see your skills developing.

# Exit Interviews

It may seem a pointless exercise to interview members of staff who are resigning from your section, after all you probably know informally why they are leaving and feel that now they have made up their mind there is nothing else to be done but wish them good luck elsewhere. However, 'exit' interviews **are** a worthwhile activity because of all the useful information which can be gained from them. Employees who are about to leave the company can comment freely, without fear of reprisal, about their place of work, the job they do and the people they work with, and it would be foolish to ignore this opportunity to gather feedback which you are unlikely to get at any other time.

The main reasons for carrying out exit interviews are as follows:

- to uncover 'background' reasons for leaving;
- to remedy high turnover;
- to discover any problems with supervisors, work or morale you may be unaware of;
- to update the job specification for the post;
- to monitor the effectiveness of your recruitment strategy – has there been a mismatch of candidate and job?
- to assess salary and benefits offered by competitors;
- to leave a good company image in the employee's mind; and
- to persuade the employee to withdraw his resignation, if appropriate.

Of course, what you learn from the interview may not always be negative: there will be many employees who are not leaving because of any dissatisfaction and who will express pleasure and fulfilment in their job and the organisation. This in itself is gratifying and useful; it is just as helpful to know where employees are satisfied as it is to detect areas of discontent.

# Preparation

## Documentation

As with any type of interview, effective preparation is essential if both you and the employee are to gain from the exercise. You should research into all relevant background information about the employee and have as many facts as possible about career and personal history at your fingertips. Personal knowledge is obviously invaluable here but this should be supplemented by an examination of the employee's file.

It is important to know about any previous jobs; employees' opinion of your company will be conditioned by experience with other employers and they will often compare conditions, unfavourably or otherwise. Also, be aware of any job changes/transfers or promotions which have taken place since they joined your organisation.

The actual interview will function as an evaluation by the employee of time spent with the company, therefore it is worth finding out as much as possible about the 'official' view of their employment. Take note of performance appraisals, pay increases and any disciplinary action taken. It will often be possible to detect earlier hints of dissatisfaction which may have a bearing on the current resignation, such as any requests for transfer or formal grievances taken up. Furnish yourself with a copy of the employee's current job description, or draw one up if necessary. It can then be discussed and up-dated, if appropriate, at the interview.

This information will give you many useful clues to the questions which should be asked in the interview. It is worth compiling a rough series of such questions beforehand so that important areas can be covered if the employee does not volunteer the information. Where there are many similar factual questions which will be asked of all resigning employees it may be appropriate to draw up a questionnaire which can be distributed beforehand and discussed and amplified at the interview. This method does make a formal analysis of results of exit interviews easier but can get in the way of free-ranging discussion, with the employee volunteering impressions of the job.

## Administration

The interview should ideally be timed to take place as soon as the employee submits notice of resignation; leaving it until the last working day after a lunchtime drink is fatal! If employees are seen as soon as possible, any remedial action to prevent them from leaving will be much more likely to succeed. Also it is much better for morale if staff feel you are interested and concerned enough about their resignation to ask them about it at the earliest opportunity.

The employee should be notified in advance of the time and location of the exit interview. It is also worthwhile explaining in broad terms the objectives and reasons for the meeting to counter any suspicions the employee may have that he is about to be carpeted. This belief will not encourage the constructive frame of mind necessary for a useful exit interview! Once exit interviews become standard practice you will not need to go too deeply into this, as further amplification can be given when you meet face to face.

Try to give some time, say two days, for employees to prepare their thoughts about what they wish to say. Staff who are ready to speak out are more likely to be helpful and informative. If you intend to use a questionnaire this is the time to distribute it. Also, inform the employee and his immediate boss of the likely duration of the interview and length of absence from work.

You should ensure a quiet room is available for the interview, free from any interruptions. It is often helpful to have a fairly informal seating arrangement for this type of interview as you want to encourage a relaxed, friendly atmosphere. Low chairs arranged around a table are better than sitting behind a desk.

You may want to combine the exit interview with other necessary administrative procedures, such as sorting out the recovery of company property, paying up of loans, return of identity cards, etc. In these circumstances you should obviously acquaint yourself with the necessary information and lead into the interview proper by getting these administrative affairs out of the way. However, it is often preferable to hold a separate meeting to deal with these matters as they do tend to cloud the real purpose of the interview and it is difficult to shift from one area of discussion to another.

## Conducting the Interview

The techniques used in an exit interview are rather different from disciplinary or recruitment interviews. An exit interview is much less of a two-way process; your object is not to impart any information but to encourage the employee to speak freely about views held on the job and the organisation. You should aim for a relaxed atmosphere, a 'tell me all about it' approach. It should be stressed that this is a normal, everyday situation which is not threatening to the employee in any way. The emphasis of the proceedings will be on eliciting information in a cordial manner and the more friendly you are the more likely it is that the employee will open up with his real views. Once you have got the employee talking you only need to ensure that the information he is volunteering is relevant.

### Opening the Interview

Your intention is to establish rapport as soon as possible so you should begin by putting the employee at ease, offering coffee and expressing regret at the resignation. Go on to outline the reasons for carrying out exit interviews (see page 79). It is important to remember that you are relying very much on the employees' good nature to co-operate in the way you require, especially as they personally will not have much to gain from any results. The benefits of any information will go to the company and remaining employees.

It is, therefore, worth being tactful and persuasive: stress how the employee can assist in re-defining the job for a new applicant and how you would value his own opinion of the type of person likely to fit the bill.

Employees are generally happy to comply and are pleased to be given the opportunity to talk about their own impressions of the job, their supervisors and work-mates. In some cases it may be the first time they have been asked for their own opinion! It is often satisfactory to be given the chance to air grievances without any fear of reprisal and in some cases it may even be difficult to stem the flow!

## Strategy

It is helpful to start with some 'lead-in' questions rather than the bold "Why are you leaving then?" Begin by asking what the employee liked most and least about the job, working conditions and company facilities. Your 'lead-in' questions should be so open that the employee will reply fully and not just with a 'yes' or 'no'. Once the employee is talking informally it should not really be necessary to ask too many direct questions.

Your prime role now is to listen and evaluate the information with the occasional steering question to keep conversation flowing or to re-direct it to relevant matters. The employee will reveal much more useful information if allowed to tell the story in his own words.

You should keep your series of standard questions handy to ensure all necessary topics are covered. The main areas you will require information about can be summarised as follows:

● all factors which influenced the employee's decision to leave the company;
● whether workload was too heavy or too light;
● an assessment of the managerial capabilities of the employee's immediate boss, e.g. did he resolve complaints, encourage co-operation, show fair treatment, explain the job properly, give praise for work well done;
● whether safety procedures were properly followed;
● whether morale on the section was good;
● whether on-the-job and specialised training were adequate;
● the employee's view of pay and benefits provided;

- any suggested improvements;
- any changes to the job description which would affect the type of person recruited as a replacement; and
- details of the employee's new job, including any factors which seem more satisfying than his current work.

If the employee does not touch upon any of these matters during the interview it will be necessary to ask directly about them. This list can obviously be adapted to include particular factors in which you are interested.

### Techniques

The most useful technique in an exit interview is the ability to listen carefully and evaluate the information being given. Once the employee is talking informally in response to your opening questions it should not be necessary to question directly too frequently. This is one interview where you do not really need to contribute a great deal but should just act as a sounding board for the interviewee. Listen carefully to what is said and express any comments you make in response in a neutral fashion. Beware of allowing your personal opinion of the events and people described to influence your attitude to the views stated and any subsequent report made.

It is also possible to influence unduly the course of events in the interview itself by letting your opinion dominate the proceedings. As the interviewer you are in a powerful position to indicate, even by body language and expression, what you want to hear from the employee, who will often then come up with responses favourable to you. For example, an interviewer can show he is not interested in the employee's complaint about lack of promotion prospects by shuffling papers, fidgeting, looking bored, staring out of the window, looking at his watch, and so on. Even the most insensitive employee will catch on pretty quickly and move on to something which does interest the interviewer, such as appreciation of training courses which he set up. Equally, the use of leading questions, such as asking "Did you ever worry about the routine

nature of your job/low pay/supervisor's bad temper?"
when the employee has not mentioned any of these
matters of his own volition, can distort the outcome.
You can, by these means, effectively plant something in
the employee's mind which will distort the picture you
are trying to build up of his true reasons for leaving the
company.

There is, of course, a thin line between this sort of
questioning and the type of probing questions you will
need to ask. Next to listening and evaluating skills,
probing is the most useful technique in an exit
interview. Your overall aim is to build up a complete
picture of the employee's attitudes towards the topics
you have identified as being most important. This is
rather like doing a jigsaw – you will pick up bits of
useful information from personnel records, from what
the employee says during the interview and also from
what he does not say!

Exit interviews are often condemned as being
notoriously unreliable because employees are reluctant
to reveal their true reasons for leaving. It is certainly
true that you may be given surface reasons which cover
up the really influential factors; that is why it is essential
to be prepared to probe behind easily produced,
seemingly convincing statements. For example, an
employee may state that he is resigning because he is
leaving the area. That may indeed be the case but there
could be many other reasons which have prompted the
decision and it is your task to find them out. It is
obviously a matter of judgement as to whether you
accept a reason as valid or decide that the true picture is
being concealed. In the latter case you will want to
probe behind the bald statement of fact, but be careful
to confine your questioning to open questions and avoid
any leading statements (as above). Ask something like,
"Apart from your decision to move from the area, are
there any comments you would like to make on the
content of your job, your supervisor or pay, etc?" If the
employee does not respond to this approach you will
have to switch to direct questioning such as "How do
you get on with your colleagues or your supervisor?"
and carry on in this vein. The interview may end up

being rather like an interrogation but, hopefully, the employee's real reasons will become apparent.

## Ending the Interview

Once all the relevant information has been obtained the interview should be ended. There is no point in letting employees carry on going over the same points, even if they feel very strongly about the problems which have prompted their resignation. Again it is a matter of assessing when you have gathered all of the useful information but, in general, if you have covered all the points in your series of questions it is time to close the meeting tactfully.

Thank the employee for his co-operation and wish him every success in his new job. It is important to end the interview on a high note, making the employee feel he has worked for a company and a manager who appreciated his work and are interested in his future. You can lead in by asking for details of the new job in a manner which will be interpreted as expressing interest rather than snooping.

It may be worth asking at this point whether the employee has any objection to a full report of the interview being made and passed on to the personnel department and/or senior management. This may seem rather like a fait accompli to the employee but it is better to be aware if there are any strong objections to certain material being made public. You may prefer to make use of this by keeping it to yourself rather than breach the employee's confidence and cause bad feeling. The employee may be persuaded that it will be more beneficial if the report is freely available to management who may be able to make changes on the strength of the information.

If the employee has specific complaints which you feel are well founded you may be prepared to commit yourself to an assurance that these will be investigated so that similar problems do not happen again. This will be particularly useful if you are trying to persuade the employee to withdraw his resignation.

# Common Problems in Exit Interviews

## Employee Resistance

You will generally find that employees are happy to co-operate in an exit interview, pleased to reflect on their time with the company and glad that someone is interested enough to find out their feelings on the matter. However, you may occasionally encounter an employee who is very resistant to the interview and makes this obvious by avoiding or refusing to answer questions. It will be pretty obvious when this is motivated by deliberate resistance rather than nerves.

The tactics outlined earlier should help, especially the explanation of the purpose and benefits of the interview and it may be worth reiterating these for further emphasis. If a person is very reluctant to open up and answers with a stream of monosyllables, it is quite likely that a serious problem is being concealed, so you should make special efforts to find this out. Indicating that you are unable to do anything about problems you are unaware of is a start and you can go on to persuade the employee to get this out of the way by asking "Is there anything in particular you would like to tell me that you are especially concerned about?" If the employee is still not prepared to say any more it may be appropriate to end the interview at this point. Express concern that you have not been able to learn what is bothering him and suggest that he thinks the matter over and comes back in a day or two. It is worth having one or even several interviews with this type of employee because there are often real grievances underlying the silence and he could be heading towards a constructive dismissal claim.

## Nerves/Fears

There are other reasons why employees are not prepared to speak out in an exit interview and, indeed, refusal to co-operate in this way is likely to be your major problem. Some employees are extremely nervous because they interpret any interview as a confrontation. Your preparatory work in giving them advance warning of the interview and setting up a friendly, relaxed environment will help to overcome this. Make it clear that you are not expecting them to account for any previous mistakes but are genuinely interested in whatever they have to tell you.

Other employees may simply be concerned about revealing too many complaints because of future references they may need from you. They will probably reason out that now they are leaving anyway their problems are behind them and there is no point in rocking the boat. If you suspect this to be the case you can counter it with reassurances. Appeal to the employee's better nature by explaining how an explanation of difficulties he has experienced can help others. Also explain that anything he tells you in an exit interview will not affect any assessment already made of him and his ability (as it should not!).


### Bitterness/Resentment

There will be some employees who are extremely bitter about some aspect of their time in the company. This will usually be as a result of a personality conflict with a supervisor or another member of staff, as difficulties with other people normally tend to generate the most violent feelings! However, it may be a refusal of promotion, a low pay increase or myriad other factors which prompt a person to feel very hard done by.

It will be very difficult for these employees to see their situation objectively or to make rational and constructive comments. You must obviously make allowances for strength of personal feeling but it is important not to let comments obviously motivated by animosity stand. Any disrespectful and offensive remarks should be checked immediately by reminding the employees where they are and to whom they are speaking. If employees have a genuine case for ill-feeling it is important to investigate, before they actually leave if possible. Otherwise if they are simply upset at what you consider to be a legitimate management action you can only express regret they feel this way but indicate that the action is taken and try to remind them of some positive aspects of their time with you.

# Follow-Up

## The Exit Interview Report

You should write up a report of the interview as soon as possible afterwards. In this way all the information recounted will be fresh in your mind and the notes can be supplemented by memory of any other matters not recorded. It is probably sensible to have a standard format for all exit interview reports, following the pattern of your series of standard questions. This will make them much less onerous to produce and also easier to compare.

The report should be headed by standard factual information about the employee: name; job title; section; date of birth and date of joining the company; current salary; and a brief career history. It may also be helpful to record the employee's main reason for leaving under this section. You can then begin the report proper by outlining all significant factors which have had a bearing on the resignation. Follow this with a summary of all the information on working conditions, safety, supervisor's ability, pay, etc. which you have gleaned from the interview. At this stage you are simply recounting the employee's impressions without any personal comment. You can then go on to record your own opinions of the employee, the interview and the validity of any criticisms/suggestions he has made. End the report with a proposed action plan arising out of the interview.

You should not be reluctant to record any problems or improvement the employee is concerned about. You may feel that his suggestions have little merit and his complaints are merely unfounded personal gripes, but nevertheless they should be considered for further investigation. Final judgement should be suspended until the matter has been looked into and you should be receptive, even to difficulties which have previously been discounted. This is particularly important if exit interviews are being carried out to remedy a high turnover of staff. It will be too late to ascribe personal inflexibility as a cause when the tenth person has left complaining about a rigid working system and the Managing Director is breathing down your neck!

It is worth considering whether the employee should see a copy of his exit interview report and sign to agree that it is an accurate assessment of what was said at the interview. This can be useful if you have to tackle a difficult supervisor or try to persuade senior management to take action on the basis of the report. It will not be possible for them to suggest that you have exaggerated or mis-reported anything an employee has told you and thus avoid taking the report seriously.

## Action

It is important to ensure that some form of action is taken as a result of carrying out an exit interview, otherwise it is just a worthless exercise. At the very least, recurring problems in certain areas should be investigated. The action plan in your exit interview report (see above) should be used to monitor any action taken and the outcome of any investigations should be noted, even if it is only a decision to maintain the status quo.

Information gleaned about changes in the job description, plus clues as to why the current job-holder was not happy or did not fit in with the section may be used to aid the recruitment process. This could mean completely re-thinking the job specification or angling recruitment towards a less qualified or more mature applicant. For example, a lathe operator may have originally persuaded you that his 10 'O' levels did not mean he would be bored with the job. However, when he resigns and tells you it is because of a lack of job fulfilment you can narrow your replacement candidates to those with fewer formal qualifications. Alternatively, a junior secretarial post which was filled by a school or college leaver may have developed into a more demanding role with the job-holder's increasing experience. You will now need to look for a more experienced person to fit the bill which will result in a more successful job match than if the original specification had been followed. This, in its turn, should mean fewer resignations and less exit interviewing!

The most important thing is to make use of the valuable information imparted to you in an exit interview and not to ignore signs of general dissatisfaction with a particular person or work procedure. If a lot of people are resigning and citing similar reasons, check out staff morale as a whole and take whatever remedial action seems necessary. This could mean something as simple as ensuring employees are given at least 24 hours' notice that they will be required to work overtime, which will improve the feeling all round and lead to fewer turnover problems.

**Analysis**

Formal analysis of the results of a series of exit interviews will probably be carried out by the personnel or administration department but the results are useful for the line manager. It might also be helpful, if you intend to carry out several interviews, to do a little basic analysis yourself as a means of getting a grip on the information.

The crucial thing to remember is that any analysis should only be carried out if it is actually going to be of practical assistance in helping you to understand why employees leave your section and to make sense of what they think about their jobs. Doing an analysis for the sake of it is pointless and time-wasting.

The sort of thing which could be done very simply would be a straightforward breakdown of all leavers into groups according to their reasons. Armed with percentages based on this breakdown, you will be in a much better position to persuade others to take action on wage differentials, working patterns or personality problems, etc. The best way of doing this is to work out a list of the major obvious reasons for resignations, for example: financial dissatisfaction/job dissatisfaction/ moving location/career progression/better offer/ personality conflict/self-employment/return to education or training/health/personal or family difficulties/ supervision/other.

These can be categorised as voluntary reasons for terminating employment and for the sake of comparison it is worth keeping records of the number of employees who leave for 'involuntary' reasons. It will not normally be appropriate to carry out a full-scale exit interview with employees who have been dismissed because, apart from other things, they will probably have been interviewed in a disciplinary context anyway. However, it may occasionally be worth asking them their opinion of various aspects of the job, if you can overcome any resentment and hostility. The major reasons for involuntary termination of employment are: retirement/pregnancy/dismissal. Dismissals may be further categorised by reason for the dismissal.

Once you have listed these categories it is generally a simple matter to assign one to each employee who leaves your department (for ease of reference you can give the categories numbers or letters to identify them). Often, of course, there is a combination of reasons why people are leaving employment but you can normally establish one overriding reason.

If you fit each employee into a particular category it is an easy task to work out percentages of employees leaving over a period of time for various reasons. This should help you to get an idea of what is actually happening and enable you to take or recommend remedial action on the basis of the information. For example, if it transpired that 56% of voluntary leavers were dissatisfied with their rates of pay you could have sufficient ammunition to persuade senior management to look again at the pay structure.

# Outside Agency Interviews

Ask a first line supervisor or manager "What would you do if a Health and Safety Inspector, official from the Department of Health and Social Security, police officer, etc. turned up on the company premises?", and the answer would probably be, "Refer them to the Safety Officer, Pay or Personnel Department, a senior manager or whoever seemed most appropriate". The chances are that the supervisor would not be in a position to deal with the person directly, and would not be required to do so. But what if he is the most senior or most appropriate person on the premises at the time? For instance if the visitor arrives outside normal office hours or if the person he needs to see is not available?

As somebody in a position of responsibility, you will be best equipped to deal with such situations if you know what sort of rights of entry the caller has, what the implications are of dealing with the matter yourself and if you know whether you can refuse to co-operate or to answer any questions put to you.

## "Halt, Who Goes There!"

If an unknown person does arrive unannounced on the premises, there are two things that should always be done in respect of them. First of all, they should be challenged as to who they are and what they are doing there. It is all too easy to assume that someone else has done that, and knows who they are and what they are about. Do not worry if that has already happened; the person concerned should be impressed with your concern for security rather than put out at having to answer the same questions again. It is always better to be safe than sorry, just in case they are up to no good. They should then be asked for proof of identity if they claim to be there in an official capacity of some kind. If they cannot produce their credentials, or you are not happy with them, ask for details of their office, department or whatever and check with them.

Having got the preliminaries out of the way, the next step will depend on who the visitor is and where he has come from.

## Health and Safety Inspectors

Of all the officials who might have occasion to visit a company's premises, the Health and Safety Inspector is probably the one with the widest powers and also the one who is most likely to turn up at an odd time, particularly if he suspects the company of operating some sort of unsafe practice and wants to catch them on the hop.

All inspectors should carry a visiting card identifying them, and should be asked to produce it. They will usually ask to see the most senior production person present, and that may well be the first line supervisor or manager if the visit takes place during the operation of a night shift. Having established who they are and what they are there for, the supervisor can always ask if they will wait until a more senior person has been contacted and arrived. If the inspector is happy to do so – fine, but it may arouse his suspicions that he is being put off and that, while he is waiting, something he should not see is being removed from sight. In such a case he may well declare his intention to carry out a tour of the premises unaccompanied, rather than await someone else's arrival. This is usually less than desirable since, as the senior person there, the supervisor should be in a position to report back fully to his bosses on what the inspector does and says. As to whether he can refuse the inspector access to the premises or require him to leave – in short the answer is "no". His powers are very far-reaching and the implications of obstructing him can be very serious.

### Their Powers

In order to ensure that the law on health and safety is being complied with, a Health and Safety Inspector has the power to do any of the following, as long as he is acting within his field of responsibility:

- enter any premises at any reasonable time (or at any time if he believes a situation is dangerous);
- bring with him any other person or any equipment or materials;
- carry out any examination or investigation he thinks necessary, including taking measurements, photographs or any other kind of recording, and he can order that the premises be left undisturbed while he does this;
- take samples of anything found on the premises, or have it dismantled or tested;
- demand to be shown any book or document he thinks necessary, not just those which have to be kept by law;
- require the use of facilities (such as an office) or obtain any help and assistance he feels he might need;
- interview and ask questions of anyone he considers appropriate; the person concerned has the right to be accompanied and is required to sign a declaration of the truth of his answers.

At the end of the day, if this does not cover all his needs, the inspector is also granted, by law, any other power which is necessary for him to enforce the law. These amount, therefore, to very wide-ranging powers indeed.

**The Supervisor's Role**

If you think that a policy of non-co-operation might be your best bet, you should think again. It is a specific offence to obstruct an inspector in any way if he is acting within his powers, whether by refusing to give him the documents he wants, by trying to prevent him asking someone questions or whatever, and could result in the individual being fined.

What you can do is ask the inspector for proof of his powers, which he should be able to produce. You can also insist on being present if the inspector has anything dismantled or tested, and the inspector must leave with you written details of anything which he takes away with him.

You may also be worried about the implications of making any sort of statement to the inspector, or of allowing others to do so. The fact is, though, that even though there is a statutory obligation to give a statement if required to do so, it is not admissible in evidence in court proceedings. Therefore, it is not possible for people to incriminate themselves by what they say – though they may be liable to prosecution for obstructing the inspector if they refuse to do so. Should an inspector wish to use what an individual tells him in court proceedings (for instance, following an accident at work) he must do as the police do and caution the individual (see page 101). In such circumstances the individual is not obliged to say anything but, if he does, he must remember that it can be used in evidence.

The supervisor should also be aware of a Health and Safety Inspector's more formal powers, namely that he can draw up an Improvement or Prohibition Notice on the spot, and serve it on a responsible person who appears to be resident or employed on the premises concerned. Again, this will probably be the most senior person present if the notice is being served on the company, and may well be the supervisor. Whatever the case, at the end of the inspector's visit, you should ask about what will happen next. Will the inspector be writing, taking any other action, or what? You should then make notes on what has happened, so that a full report can be made to your superiors.

## Inland Revenue

While there cannot be too many people who welcome the prospect of a visitor from the Inland Revenue, tax officials are a fact of life and they may well turn up on your company's premises from time to time.

For instance, if they are not provided with a tax return, or are not satisfied with the return, they may serve a notice on the company requiring copies of the relevant accounts to be delivered to them or the notice might require all relevant books, accounts and other documents to be made available for inspection by a tax official.

In the – hopefully rare – event that your company refuses to pay its taxes, the tax collector may, after obtaining a warrant signed by the General Commissioners of Inland Revenue, break open any house or premises in order to seize goods, equipment, etc. to the value of the tax owed.

However, most contact with the Inland Revenue will be much less dramatic than this. In practice, most companies find that the attentions of tax officers are confined to occasional audits, for instance to check that PAYE procedures are being followed properly. While they have powers to enter and inspect premises at any reasonable time they will, in almost every case, make an appointment to ensure that they are able to see the right company official. After all, if they turn up one day when the people who are responsible for tax matters are all away on holiday, it is unlikely that anyone will be able to help them since all the documents they want to see are likely to be under lock and key!

In such a case, they should politely be asked to come back at a more convenient, mutually agreed, time.

## Department of Health and Social Security

DHSS Inspectors have the following powers under the 1975 Social Security Act:

- to enter at all reasonable times any premises in which the inspector has reasonable grounds to believe people are employed, or where an employment agency operates;

- to carry out whatever examination or inquiry he thinks necessary to ensure the provisions of the legislation are being complied with, or to investigate the circumstances of an industrial injury which has given or may give rise to a claim;

- to examine, either alone or in the presence of someone else (whichever he thinks fit), anyone on the premises;

- to exercise any other powers necessary to ensure compliance with the legislation.

Initially, these powers were conferred to enable the inspectors to check that national insurance contributions were being properly deducted, recorded and paid over to the DHSS. However, nowadays inspectors are also interested in the administration and payment of Statutory Sick Pay by employers and, to some extent, this may mean that visits from them are more likely. In practice, they are usually fairly friendly and helpful and are only likely to appear on the premises at a time when they think they will be able to gain access to the records and people they want to see. It would, therefore, be unusual for a supervisor to have to deal with them personally, but you should still be aware of the fact that they do have statutory powers which can be enforced if they choose.

Every inspector should carry a certificate of his appointment and can be required to produce it in order to gain access to the premises. Once admitted, they can demand to see any documents or obtain any information they think necessary to check that the legislation is being complied with. If anyone wilfully delays or obstructs them in the exercise of any of their powers, they can be fined on summary conviction. The occupier of the premises is obviously bound by this duty but so would be a supervisor or any other employee, since 'servants or agents' of the occupier can also be held liable. Similarly, it is an offence to refuse to answer an inspector's questions but note that (unlike with the Health and Safety Inspector) no one can be required to answer any questions or give any evidence which might incriminate him.

## Wages Inspectors

For those companies operating in an industry or employing workers covered by a Wages Council Order, a visit from the Wages Inspector is always a possibility. Their powers are laid down in the Wages Act 1986 and are as follows:

- at all reasonable times, to enter any premises where

an employer to whom a wages order applies carries on his business:

● to inspect wages sheets or other records of wages kept by the employer;

● to inspect and copy any list of homeworkers or demand information as to the names, addresses and payment details of homeworkers;

● to interview, either alone or in the presence of someone else (whichever he thinks fit), any employee covered by a wages order, and require him to sign a declaration as to the truth of his answers.

As usual, every Wages Inspector should carry a certificate of appointment and can be required to produce it. Again, it is an offence to obstruct an inspector in the carrying out of his duties, which can result in a fine on summary conviction. However, as with the DHSS Inspector, no one can be required to give any information which might incriminate him.


## Data Protection Registrar

The Data Protection Act 1984 is not implemented in full until the end of 1987. The powers of entry and inspection of the Data Protection Registrar (or his officers) must be taken into account. Remember, though, that the Act only applies to computerised information – not to manual records.

Unlike the officials mentioned so far, the Data Protection Registrar is not granted automatic powers in the legislation; they are conferred on him only when he succeeds in getting a warrant issued. If he just turns up on the premises he can be refused entry or access to information if you are not happy to deal with him and no more senior people are available. At that point you will not be committing any offence. Obviously, the Registrar may then take steps to get a warrant issued which will confer powers of entry and inspection on him. First of all, though, he must:

● give the occupier seven days' notice demanding access to the premises;

- demand access at a reasonable hour and be unreasonably refused; and
- after the refusal, notify the occupier that he is applying for a warrant.

Only if the case is urgent will these conditions be waived.

This means that, even if the Registrar has given seven days' notice of his intention to visit the premises, if you refuse either to allow him entry or to co-operate with him, again no offence will have been committed although, obviously, it would be more sensible to co-operate other than in exceptional circumstances.

Once a warrant has been issued, however, the situation is rather different. It will authorise the Registrar or his officers to:

- enter the premises at any time within seven days of the date of the warrant;
- search them;
- inspect, examine, operate and test any data equipment found there;
- inspect and seize any documents or anything else considered as evidence that an offence has been committed.

A warrant will only be issued by a judge if he is satisfied that an offence under the Act has been or is being committed, or that any of the data protection principles are being broken. However, once issued, the person who executes the warrant must usually do so at a reasonable time but can use any reasonable force which is necessary. If the occupier of the premises is present he must be shown the warrant and given a copy of it, and can demand a receipt for anything seized by the Registrar.

Anyone who intentionally obstructs the Registrar in the execution of a warrant, or fails to help him in any way which he reasonably requires, will be committing an offence and may be liable to a fine on conviction.

# The Police

One other group of visitors who may turn up on the premises at any time are the police. As with the Data Protection Registrar, strictly speaking their rights of entry are largely dependent on possession of a warrant. Otherwise, unless they are seeking to enter premises because they believe a crime is being committed there at the time, you could refuse them access without necessarily committing an offence. What you must be wary of, however, is obstructing them in the carrying out of their duty, e.g. apprehending an offender who they believe to be on the premises, as that would be an offence. In practice, whether there is a possibility of obstruction or not, it is always advisable to co-operate with the police and, unless you have reason to believe they are not who they say they are, you should allow them into the premises.

When it comes to answering questions, it will depend largely on the police officers' reasons for being there. If they are trying to discover whether an offence has been committed or who has committed it, they are entitled to question anyone – whether or not they are under suspicion – who they think might be able to provide useful information. Every individual is under a duty to help the police discover and apprehend offenders and, again, may be guilty of obstruction if he refuses to answer. If an individual has been charged with an offence, or if it is suspected that he may have committed it, he must be cautioned by the police before being asked any questions, in the following terms:
"You are not obliged to say anything unless you wish to do so but what you say may be put into writing and given in evidence".
That person need not then say anything, and may wish to consult a solicitor.

# All and Sundry

Those groups of people described above are the ones most likely to appear at the company's gates with any sort of legal right of entry or enquiry. Any other visitors need only be admitted and shown co-operation if they are there at the company's request or with its permission. This includes such official sounding visitors as solicitors, ACAS officials, full time union representatives, etc. There is no legal obligation to allow them access to the premises and, if they refuse to leave, the police can be called to deal with them as trespassers. Whether it is advisable to do this is another matter, but if you do not wish to deal with such visitors until a more senior person is present, you have every right to require them to come back at another time.

The wisdom of treating customers or suppliers of the company as trespassers is particularly doubtful – especially if they have come to complain! In such circumstances, if the person most appropriate for them to see is not available, the best thing to do is to be as conciliatory as possible, particularly if you do not know the merits of their case! Explain that you cannot help but that if they would like to come back later they will be able to see someone who can. Better still, take down all the details and tell them someone will contact them as soon as possible – then make sure that they do.

No matter who arrives unannounced on the premises, for the supervisor or manager who is the most senior person around and has to deal with the visitors on the spot, the main points to remember are:

- challenge them and ask for proof of identity;
- if in doubt as to their right of entry, powers, etc. ask for proof;
- make a note of all that happens and is said; and
- contact a senior manager or the most appropriate person as soon as possible with the information.

# Index

This index is divided into eight parts for the convenience of readers. The first part refers to the general principles of interviewing, while the remaining seven parts relate to the types of interview covered in the book, i.e. selection, appraisal, disciplinary, grievance, counselling, exit and outside agency interviews.

## General Principles

## Selection Interviews

## Appraisal Interviews

# Disciplinary Interviews

# Grievance Interviews

## Counselling Interviews